RENAL DIET COOKBOOK FOR BEGINNERS

CW00523558

1500 Days of Easy-to-Prepare and Delicious Recipes Low in Potassium, Phosphorus, and Sodium to Reduce Your Kidney Workload with a 31-Day Smart Meal Plan.

Erica Diason

© Copyright 2022 by Erica Diason - All rights reserved.

This document is geared towards providing exact and reliable information in regard to the topic and issue covered.

- From a Declaration of Principles which was accepted and approved equally by a Committee of the American Bar Association and a Committee of Publishers and Associations.

In no way is it legal to reproduce, duplicate, or transmit any part of this document in either electronic means or in printed format. All rights reserved.

The information provided herein is stated to be truthful and consistent, in that any liability, in terms of inattention or otherwise, by any usage or abuse of any policies, processes, or directions contained within is the solitary and utter responsibility of the recipient reader. Under no circumstances will any legal responsibility or blame be held against the publisher for any reparation, damages, or monetary loss due to the information herein, either directly or indirectly.

Respective authors own all copyrights not held by the publisher.

The information herein is offered for informational purposes solely and is universal as so. The presentation of the information is without contract or any type of guarantee assurance.

The trademarks that are used are without any consent, and the publication of the trademark is without permission or backing by the trademark owner. All trademarks and brands within this book are for clarifying purposes only and are owned by the owners themselves, not affiliated with this document.

Table of Contents

INTRODUCTION 8

MEDICAL CONSULTATION WITH A NUTRITIONIST OR NEPHROLOGIST ABOUT YOUR DIALYSIS 9

THE ROLE OF PHOSPHOROUS IN OUR BODY 10
POTASSIUM 10
SODIUM 10

IMPORTANCE OF PREVENTION 12

EAT RIGHT AND LOSE EXCESS WEIGHT 12
EXERCISE 12
TRY NOT TO SMOKE 12
BE CAUTIOUS OF GLUCOSE LEVELS 12
FATTY INTAKE 12
STARCHES 12
LIMIT PROTEIN INTAKE 13
FLUID INTAKE 13

DIFFERENT KIDNEY DISEASES 14

A BRIEF OVERVIEW OF CHRONIC RENAL DISEASE 14
THE SIGNS AND SYMPTOMS 14

IMPORTANCE OF REDUCING THE NUMBER OF PROTEIN FOODS 16

HIGH-CALORIE INTAKE 16
CARBOHYDRATES 16
OILS 16
RESTRICTION OF PROTEIN INTAKE 16
FLUID INTAKE 17
WHY SHOULD CHRONIC KIDNEY PATIENTS TAKE PRECAUTIONS ABOUT FLUID INTAKE? 17
WHAT PRECAUTIONS SHOULD CHRONIC KIDNEY PATIENTS TAKE TO CONTROL FLUID INTAKE? 17
WHAT IS THE RECOMMENDED AMOUNT OF FLUID FOR PATIENTS WITH CHRONIC KIDNEY DISEASE? 17
WHY SHOULD CHRONIC KIDNEY PATIENTS KEEP A RECORD OF THEIR DAILY WEIGHT? 17
USEFUL TIPS FOR RESTRICTING FLUID INTAKE 17

GUIDELINES TO LIMIT SALT 18

KEEP A FOOD DIARY 18
READ FOOD LABELS 18
CHECK FOOD LABELS TO AVOID 18
FLAVOR FOODS WITH SPICES AND HERBS RATHER THAN SHOP-BOUGHT DRESSINGS AND CONDIMENTS 18
KEEP UP YOUR APPOINTMENTS WITH YOUR DOCTOR OR NEPHROLOGIST 18
MONITOR DRINK AND FLUID INTAKE 18
MEASURE PORTION SIZES 18
SUBSTITUTION TIPS 18
OTHER ADVICE 19

FOODS TO AVOID AND WHAT TO EAT 20

FOOD TO EAT 20
SODIUM AND ITS ROLE IN THE BODY 20
POTASSIUM AND ITS ROLE IN THE BODY 21
PHOSPHORUS AND ITS ROLE IN THE BODY 21
PROTEIN 22
FOOD TO AVOID 22
FOOD WITH HIGH SODIUM CONTENT 22
FOOD WITH A HIGH POTASSIUM LEVEL 22
FOODS WITH HIGH PHOSPHORUS 22
RENAL DIET SHOPPING LIST 23
VEGETABLES 23
FRUITS 23
FRESH MEAT, SEAFOOD, AND POULTRY 24
MILK, EGGS, AND DAIRY 24

RENAL DIET IN 4 SEASONS OF THE YEAR 25

SPRING 25
SUMMER 25
FALL 25
WINTER 25

BREAKFAST RECIPES 27

1. TURKEY AND SPINACH SCRAMBLE ON MELBA TOAST 27
2. CHEESY SCRAMBLED EGGS WITH FRESH HERBS 27
3. BULGUR, COUSCOUS, AND BUCKWHEAT CEREAL 28
4. BLUEBERRY MUFFINS 28
5. BUCKWHEAT AND GRAPEFRUIT PORRIDGE 28
6. EGG AND VEGGIE MUFFINS 29
7. BERRY CHIA WITH YOGURT 29
8. ARUGULA EGGS WITH CHILI PEPPERS 29
9. EGGPLANT CHICKEN SANDWICH 30

10.	EGGS IN TOMATO RINGS	30
11.	CHORIZO BOWL WITH CORN	30
12.	PANZANELLA SALAD	31
13.	POACHED EGG WITH ASPARAGUS	31
14.	EGG DROP SOUP	32
15.	RASPBERRY OVERNIGHT PORRIDGE	32
16.	SUMMER VEGGIE OMELET	32
17.	BREAKFAST MAPLE SAUSAGE	32
18.	FAST MICROWAVE EGG SCRAMBLE	33
19.	AMERICAN BLUEBERRY PANCAKES	33
20.	MEXICAN SCRAMBLED EGGS IN TORTILLA	33
21.	EGG WHITE AND BROCCOLI OMELET	34

APPETIZERS RECIPES 35

22.	CHEESY BROCCOLI BITES	35
23.	EASY CAPRESE SKEWERS	35
24.	GRILLED TOFU WITH SESAME SEEDS	35
25.	KALE CHIPS	36
26.	SIMPLE DEVILED EGGS	36
27.	SAUTÉED COLLARD GREENS AND CABBAGE	36
28.	ROASTED DELICATA SQUASH WITH THYME	37
29.	ROASTED ASPARAGUS AND RED PEPPERS	37
30.	TARRAGON SPRING PEAS	37
31.	BUTTER-ORANGE YAMS	37
32.	ROASTED TOMATO BRUSSELS SPROUTS	38
33.	GREEN BEANS IN OVEN	38
34.	CREAM OF WATERCRESS	38
35.	BAKED GARLIC	39
36.	MEXICAN NIBBLES	39
37.	CREAMY CUCUMBER	40
38.	DILL NIBBLES	40
39.	CRAB-STUFFED CELERY LOGS	40
40.	BARBECUE MEATBALLS	41
41.	HOLIDAY CHEESE BALL	41
42.	HULA MEATBALLS	42
43.	HOLIDAY TUNA BALL	42

LUNCH RECIPES 43

44.	CRISPY LEMON CHICKEN	43
45.	MEXICAN STEAK TACOS	43
46.	BEER PORK RIBS	44
47.	MEXICAN CHORIZO SAUSAGE	44
48.	ITALIAN MEATBALLS	44
49.	EGGPLANT CASSEROLE	45
50.	MEXICAN STYLE BURRITOS	45
51.	PIZZA WITH CHICKEN AND PESTO	45
52.	SHRIMP QUESADILLA	46
53.	GRILLED CORN ON THE COB	46

54.	COUSCOUS WITH VEGGIES	47
55.	EASY EGG SALAD	47
56.	CUCUMBER SANDWICH	47
57.	PIZZA PITAS	48
58.	TURKEY PINWHEELS	48
59.	CHICKEN TACOS	48
60.	CIABATTA ROLLS WITH CHICKEN PESTO	49
61.	MARINATED SHRIMP PASTA SALAD	49
62.	PEANUT BUTTER AND JELLY GRILLED SANDWICH	49
63.	GRILLED ONION AND PEPPER JACK GRILLED CHEESE SANDWICH	50
64.	LETTUCE WRAPS WITH CHICKEN	50

DINNER RECIPES 51

65.	SEAFOOD CASSEROLE	51
66.	EGGPLANT AND RED PEPPER SOUP	51
67.	GROUND BEEF AND RICE SOUP	52
68.	COUSCOUS BURGERS	52
69.	PORK SOUVLAKI	53
70.	BAKED FLOUNDER	53
71.	PERSIAN CHICKEN	53
72.	BEEF CHILI	54
73.	PORK MEATLOAF	54
74.	CHICKEN STEW	55
75.	GREEN TUNA SALAD	55
76.	ROASTED CHICKEN AND VEGETABLES	56
77.	SIRLOIN MEDALLIONS, GREEN SQUASH, AND PINEAPPLE	56
78.	CHICKEN AND SAVORY RICE	57
79.	SALMON AND GREEN BEANS	57
80.	BAKED MACARONI AND CHEESE	57
81.	KOREAN PEAR SALAD	58
82.	BEEF ENCHILADAS	58
83.	CHICKEN AND BROCCOLI CASSEROLE	59
84.	FETA BEAN SALAD	59
85.	SALMON MAYO SANDWICH	60

FISH AND SEAFOOD RECIPES 61

86.	BAKED FISH À LA MUSHROOMS	61
87.	SHRIMP AND ASPARAGUS LINGUINE	61
88.	OLD FASHIONED SALMON SOUP	62
89.	SHRIMP IN GARLIC SAUCE	62
90.	TUNA TWIST	63
91.	EGGPLANT SEAFOOD CASSEROLE	63
92.	HALIBUT WITH LEMON CAPER SAUCE	63
93.	JAMBALAYA	64
94.	SHRIMP SZECHUAN	64
95.	SHRIMP SCAMPI LINGUINE	65

96.	GRILLED SHRIMP WITH CUCUMBER LIME SALSA	65
97.	CRAB CAKES WITH LIME SALSA	65
98.	SWEET GLAZED SALMON	66
99.	HERB-CRUSTED BAKED HADDOCK	66
100.	BAKED COD WITH SALSA	67
101.	CILANTRO-LIME FLOUNDER	67
102.	COOKED TILAPIA WITH MANGO SALSA	68
103.	CILANTRO AND CHILI INFUSED SWORDFISH	68
104.	CITRUS TUNA CEVICHE	68
105.	BAKED TROUT	69
106.	CURRIED FISH CAKES	69

VEGETARIAN AND VEGAN RECIPES — 70

107.	SAUTÉED GREEN BEANS	70
108.	GARLICKY PENNE PASTA WITH ASPARAGUS	70
109.	GARLIC MASHED POTATOES	70
110.	GINGER GLAZED CARROTS	71
111.	CARROT-APPLE CASSEROLE	71
112.	CREAMY SHELLS WITH PEAS	71
113.	DOUBLE-BOILED STEWED POTATOES	72
114.	DOUBLE-BOILED COUNTRY STYLE FRIED POTATOES	72
115.	BROCCOLI-ONION LATKES	73
116.	CRANBERRY CABBAGE	73
117.	CAULIFLOWER RICE	73
118.	SPICY MUSHROOM STIR-FRY	74
119.	CURRIED VEGGIES AND RICE	74
120.	SPICY VEGGIE PANCAKES	74
121.	EGG AND VEGGIE FAJITAS	75
122.	VEGETABLE BIRYANI	75
123.	PESTO PASTA SALAD	76
124.	BARLEY BLUEBERRY AVOCADO SALAD	76
125.	PASTA WITH CREAMY BROCCOLI SAUCE	77
126.	ASPARAGUS FRIED RICE	77
127.	VEGETARIAN TACO SALAD	78

SALAD RECIPES — 79

128.	GRAPES JICAMA SALAD	79
129.	BUTTERSCOTCH APPLE SALAD	79
130.	CRANBERRY SLAW	79
131.	BALSAMIC BEET SALAD	80
132.	EGG CELERY SALAD	80
133.	CHICKEN ORANGE SALAD	80
134.	ALMOND PASTA SALAD	81
135.	PINEAPPLE BERRY SALAD	81
136.	CABBAGE PEAR SALAD	82
137.	BRIE AND APPLE SALAD	82
138.	FARFALLE CONFETTI SALAD	82
139.	TARRAGON AND PEPPER PASTA SALAD	83

140.	BEET FETA SALAD	83
141.	CREAMED CHICKEN SALAD	83
142.	CHICKEN CRANBERRY SAUCE SALAD	84
143.	CUCUMBER-CARROT SALAD	84
144.	MEDITERRANEAN COUSCOUS SALAD	85
145.	JICAMA AND CARROT SALAD WITH HONEY-LIME DRESSING	85
146.	EASY CARAMEL APPLE SALAD	86
147.	PINEAPPLE SHRIMP SALAD	86

SEASONAL RECIPES — 87

148.	5 INGREDIENTS PASTA	87
149.	PLANT-BASED KETO LO MEIN	87
150.	VEGGIE NOODLES	87
151.	STIR FRY NOODLES	88
152.	SPICY SWEET CHILI VEGGIE NOODLES	88
153.	CREAMY VEGAN MUSHROOM PASTA	88
154.	VEGAN CHINESE NOODLES	89
155.	VEGETABLE PENNE PASTA	89
156.	CREAMY PUMPKIN PASTA	90
157.	BAKE PASTA WITH CASHEW CREAM	90
158.	CREAMY SPINACH PASTA	91
159.	CANNELLINI PESTO SPAGHETTI	91
160.	COLD ORANGE SOBA NOODLES	91
161.	CRISPY TOFU AND VEGETABLE NOODLES	92
162.	INDONESIA GREEN NOODLE SALAD	93
163.	KIMCHI GREEN RICE NOODLE SALAD	93
164.	LEMONY BROCCOLI PENNE	93
165.	PONZU PEA RICE NOODLE SALAD	94
166.	SHIITAKE AND BEAN SPROUT RAMEN	94
167.	CABBAGE ROTELLE PROVENÇALE	95
168.	SHIITAKE UDON NOODLES	95

DESSERTS AND SNACKS RECIPES — 96

169.	LEMON MERINGUE PIE	96
170.	FRESH FRUIT DESSERT CUPS	96
171.	CARAMEL-CENTERED COOKIES	97
172.	LOW-SODIUM LB. CAKE	97
173.	DESSERT PIZZA	98
174.	LEMON BARS	98
175.	BAKED PINEAPPLE	99
176.	KIDNEY-FRIENDLY VANILLA ICE CREAM	99
177.	QUICK CUPCAKES	99
178.	PEPPERMINT CRUNCH COOKIES	99
179.	SESAME CRACKERS	100
180.	VEGGIE SNACK	100
181.	HEALTHY SPICED NUTS	100
182.	VINEGAR AND SALT KALE CHIPS	101

183.	Carrot and Parsnips French Fries	101
184.	Apple and Strawberry Snack	101
185.	Candied Macadamia Nuts	102
186.	Cinnamon Apple Chips	102
187.	Lemon Pops	102
188.	Easy No-Bake Coconut Cookies	103
189.	Roasted Chili-Vinegar Peanuts	103

JUICE AND SMOOTHIE — **104**

190.	Holiday Cider	104
191.	Carrot Peach Water	104
192.	Papaya Mint Water	104
193.	Raspberry Cucumber Smoothie	105
194.	Sunny Pineapple Smoothie	105
195.	Mango Cheesecake Smoothie	105
196.	Hot Cocoa	105
197.	Rice Milk	106
198.	Almond Milk	106
199.	Cucumber and Lemon-Flavored Water	106
200.	Blueberry Smoothie	106
201.	Healthy Green Smoothie	107
202.	Carrot Orange Ginger Smoothie	107
203.	Cherry Limeade Smoothie	107
204.	Layered Smoothie	107
205.	Green Apple Orange Spice	108
206.	Maple Fig Smoothie	108
207.	Mint Protein: Smoothie	108
208.	Peachy Keen Smoothie	109
209.	Pear Basil Citrus Smoothie	109
210.	Chocolate Mint Smoothie	109

PUDDINGS AND CAKES — **110**

211.	Vegan Chocolate Peanut Butter Cheesecake	110
212.	Vegan Corn Cake	110
213.	Strawberry Biscuit Cake	110
214.	Potato and Mushroom Cake	111
215.	Azteca Cake	111
216.	Carrot and Tofu Cake	112
217.	Carrot Cake	112
218.	Orange and Chocolate Cake	112
219.	Tofu and Chocolate Mousse	113

220.	Vegan Chocolate Pudding	113
221.	Spice Cake	114
222.	Lemon Cake	114
223.	Green Tea Pudding	114
224.	Dates and Rice Pudding	115
225.	Chocolate and Avocado Mousse	115
226.	Cool Avocado Pudding	115
227.	Mango Coconut Cheesecake	116
228.	Coconut Chia Pudding	116
229.	Avocado Blueberry Cheesecake	116
230.	Mango Coconut Pudding	117

ALTERNATIVE INFUSIONS AND HERBAL TEAS — **118**

231.	Peppermint Tea	118
232.	Lavender Tea	118
233.	Rose chamomile Tea	118
234.	Hibiscus Green Tea	119
235.	Flax Seed Tea	119
236.	Basil Leaves Tea	119
237.	Guava Tea	119
238.	Ginger Onion Tea	120
239.	Turmeric Tea	120
240.	Poppy Seeds Tea	120
241.	Elderflower Tea	121
242.	Hibiscus Raspberry Green Tea	121
243.	Fennel Tea	121
244.	Blackberry Tea	122
245.	Luscious Lemon Tea	122
246.	Morning Turmeric Tonic	122
247.	Licorice Tea for Energy Boost	122
248.	Stress Relief Tea	123
249.	Powerhouse Green Tea	123
250.	Lemon Ginger Tea	123

31-DAYS MEAL PLAN — **124**

MEASUREMENT COVERAGE CHART — **127**

CONCLUSION — **128**

ALPHABETICAL RECIPE INDEX — **129**

INTRODUCTION

Many individuals find themselves searching for a new diet to try and help with their weight, health, and overall feeling of well-being. But what most people don't realize is that there are different types of diets out there. Choosing the right type is vital to helping someone reach their goals without hindering them in any way.

A renal diet is a very common type of diet that many individuals follow. It is based on what can and cannot be consumed by those suffering from kidney disorders. Contrary to popular belief, the renal diet doesn't make someone eat bland foods. Those who want to follow them can find several delicious and flavorful recipes on cookbooks or the internet. Whether someone wants to eat for health reasons or on a diet, the renal diet is a healthy choice.

The first step is to follow the renal diet based on what one's kidney function is rather than if they are following an eating plan. From there, individuals begin to cut down on their daily protein intake through food choices.

The renal diet has many benefits that can easily persuade someone to start following it. Some of these benefits include helping improve kidney function, aiding in weight loss, lowering blood pressure, lowering uric acid levels within the body, and preventing kidney stone formation.

The renal diet doesn't limit the kinds of food that can be eaten at all. Many delicious and high-protein foods can be eaten on this diet. The foods that should be avoided contain high amounts of fat, salt, and sugar. Poultry and fish make up a large percentage of the recommended daily intake.

For those who love to eat meat, there is no need to worry about the renal diet limiting this type of food in any way.

The renal diet focuses on protein intake and nutrients such as minerals and amino acids. Several people who follow this kind of diet say they feel more energetic and better concentrate when eating foods rich in these nutrients.

The renal diet is also very helpful in lowering cholesterol levels within the body. There are many cases where people who follow the renal diet have reduced their levels by at least 25%. This can help with blocking arteries that can cause heart disease.

This guide is for those individuals that are starting on their diet journey. It's dedicated to the step-by-step process of tackling kidney problems, which can arise because of too much salt in one's diet.

A low protein diet can be used with a higher protein food if one's kidneys allow it. Based on the renal diet, the options for a low protein diet are unlimited. But the most important thing with this type of diet is communicating with a doctor before starting a low protein diet.

This guide will teach the reader the proper ways to transition their diet into healthier and more beneficial for their body.

One of the most useful tips to help people understand renal diets is to break down what happens when it's gone wrong. Low protein should last no longer than 2 weeks maximum until it's gone right again.

Make sure you do comprehensive research on your kidney problems. It's best to consult the doctor regarding any of your concerns.

MEDICAL CONSULTATION WITH A NUTRITIONIST OR NEPHROLOGIST ABOUT YOUR DIALYSIS

The renal diet is designed to convey respite to patients with deliberate or injured renal functions and chronic kidney diseases. There is no single type of renal diet because requirements of the renal diet and restrictions need to match the patient's needs and be based on what the doctor prescribed for the patient's overall health.

However, all forms of renal diet have one thing in common: to improve your renal functions, bring some relief to your kidneys, and prevent kidneys disease in patients with numerous risk factors, altogether improving your overall health and well-being. The grocery list we have provided should help you get hold of which groceries you should introduce to your diet and which groups of food should be avoided to improve your kidneys' performance, so you can start shopping for your new lifestyle.

You don't need to shop for many different types of groceries all at once, as it is always better to use fresh produce. However, frozen food also makes a good alternative when fresh fruit and vegetables are not available.

Remember to treat canned goods as suggested and recommended in the portion and drain excess liquid from the canned food.

For the renal diet recommended in our guide, this form of kidney-friendly dietary regimen offers a solution in the form of low-sodium and low-potassium meals and groceries, which is why we are also offering simple and easy renal diet recipes. This dietary plan is compiled for all renal system failure stages unless the doctor recommends a different treatment by allowing or expelling some of the groceries listed in our ultimate grocery list for renal patients.

Before we get to cooking and changing your lifestyle from the very core with the idea of improving your health, you need to get familiar with renal diet basics to help you improve your kidney's health by lowering sodium and potassium intake.

The CKD has no cure, but this disease is completely manageable. Lifestyle changes can help slow the disease's development and evade symptoms that naturally begin to occur as the disease advances. These diet and régime variations can even advance your general health and help you manage associated conditions. When you begin making changes to your food and daily habits, you will also notice an improvement in these associated conditions, including hypertension and diabetes.

You can have a healthy, long, and happy life while managing this disease. Making proper changes early on can slow the progression of any adverse symptoms for several years:

- Stage 1: Slight kidney damage, and usually no symptoms. (eGFR > 90 mL)
- Stage 2: Mild damage in kidneys (eGFR = 60–89 mL)
- Stage 3: Moderate damage in kidneys (eGFR = 30–59 mL)
- Stage 4: Severe damage in kidneys (eGFR = 15–29 mL)
- Stage 5: Kidney failure/End-stage CKD (GFR < 15 mL)

The Role of Phosphorous in Our Body

Phosphorous contributes to keep our bones healthy and develop them. Phosphorous helps in muscle movement, develops the connective tissue and organs. When we eat food that contains phosphorous, the small intestines store it to build our bones. A well-functioning kidney can get rid of the extra phosphorous in the body, but a damaged one cannot do so. So renal patients must watch how much phosphorous they are consuming.

Though phosphorous helps develop bones, it can also weaken the bones by extracting calcium if too much phosphorous is consumed. The calcium removed from the bones gets deposited in blood vessels, the heart, eyes, and lungs, causing severe health problems.

The proper knowledge of high phosphorous food is required to balance phosphorous for a renal patient. Red meat, milk, fast foods like burgers, pizzas, fries, fizzy drinks that are colored, and canned fish and seeds are relatively high in phosphorous.

Packaged food or canned food also, is high in phosphorous. Therefore, read the labels before you purchase any canned goods from the supermarket.

Phosphorous binders are an excellent way to keep your phosphorous intake to a minimum. If you ask you your dietitian, they will give you an excellent phosphorous binder, which you can follow to track how much you can and should consume.

Potassium

Potassium maintains the balance of electrolytes and fluid in our bloodstream. It also regulates our heartbeat and contributes to our muscle function. You can find potassium in many fruits, vegetables, and meat. Besides, it also exists in our bodies. A healthy kidney keeps the required potassium in our body and removes the excess through urine.

A damaged kidney is not capable of removing potassium anymore. Hyperkalemia is a condition when you have too much potassium in the blood. Hyperkalemia can cause slow pulse, weak muscles, irregular heart rate, heart attack, and death.

To control your daily potassium intake, count every ingredient's potassium level. It would help consult a renal expert dietitian, as they know which ingredient would work best for your condition. Food like avocado, beans, spinach, fish, bananas, and potatoes are very high in potassium. Even if you eat these ingredients, try to divide the serving in half and eat a small one.

Do not eat these high potassium ingredients every single day. There are many low potassium foods available, and pick them when you are making your meal plan. Fresh ingredients are always better than the frozen kind. To keep track of your potassium intake throughout the day, keep a personal food journal where you can input everything and reflect when you need to.

Sodium

A renal patient must cut down on daily sodium and potassium intake to keep their kidney at rest. Sodium and salt are not interchangeable. People have a misconception that salt is the only grocery item containing sodium, but other natural foods are high in sodium. Salt is a mixture of chloride and sodium. Canned foods and processed foods have a large amount of sodium in them.

Our body has three significant electrolytes, sodium, potassium, and chloride. Sodium regulates blood vessels and blood pressure, muscle contraction, nerve function, acid balance in the blood, and keeps the balance of fluid in the body! The kidney usually excretes the toxin in our body, but a damaged kidney cannot eliminate the extra sodium in our body.

So, when a renal patient consumes too much sodium, it gets stored in the blood vessels and bloodstream. This storage of sodium can lead to feeling thirsty all the time. It is a bit problematic as kidney patients must limit their fluid intake. It can cause edema, high blood pressure, breathlessness, and even heart failure. So, a renal patient must always limit their sodium intake. The average limit is 150 mg per snack and 400 mg per meal.

Patients who struggle with kidney health issues, going through kidney dialysis, and having renal impairments need to undergo medical treatment and change their eating habits and lifestyle to improve the situation.

The first thing to changing your lifestyle is knowing how your kidney functions and how different foods can trigger different kidney function reactions. Certain nutrients affect your kidney directly. Nutrients like sodium, protein, phosphate, and potassium are the risky ones. You cannot omit them altogether from your diet, but you need to limit or minimize their intake as much as possible. You cannot leave out essential nutrients like protein from your diet, but you need to count how much protein you have per day. It is essential to keep balance in your muscles and maintaining a good functioning kidney.

A profound change in kidney patients is measuring how much fluid they are drinking. It is a crucial change in every kidney patient, and you must adapt to this new eating habit. Too much water or any other form of liquid can disrupt your kidney function. How much fluid you can consume depends on the condition of your kidney.

IMPORTANCE OF PREVENTION

Being diagnosed with chronic kidney disease is frightening, but you can take steps to keep away from dialysis when you discover the symptoms in the beginning. If you work intimately with your PCP, the odds are high you can, in any case, appreciate a refreshing personal satisfaction with kidney disease.

Following excellent health practices and evading dialysis, remaining at work, and understanding social exercises are ways individuals can feel responsible for their condition. Notwithstanding doing everything physically and medicinally conceivable to maintain a strategic distance from dialysis, having an occupation with medical coverage gives security that pays, and medical advantages will be accessible. Here are portions of the means to take to maintain a strategic distance from the beginning of dialysis.

Eat Right and Lose Excess Weight

Consistently make sure to know about serving sizes. It's what you eat that includes calories, yet also how much. Make sure to follow a smart dieting plan that consists of an assortment of nourishments as you get in shape.

Exercise

Most dialysis patients accept they can't work out. In all certainty, most dialysis patients can work out. Numerous renal patients depict regular exercise as the principal action that made them feel "normal" again after beginning dialysis medications. Regardless of whether it is just for a brief timeframe every day, movement allows patients with persistent kidney disease to feel good, more grounded, and more responsible for their health.

Medicinal experts working in renal recovery have demonstrated that an ordinary exercise program, anyway restricted, not just upgrades an individual's potential for physical action, also improves the general personal satisfaction for individuals on dialysis. Exercise can also help the kidney symptoms patient recover the function to perform activities they were delighted in before being analyzed.

Try Not to Smoke

In case you smoke, there is, in all likelihood, no other choice you can make to help your health more than stopping. At the same time, an ongoing examination found that smokers lose ten years of life expectancy at any rate than people who never smoked.

Be Cautious of Glucose Levels

For good preventive health, cut back on soda pop, treats, and sugary baked goods, making glucose rise. If you have diabetes, this can hurt your heart, kidneys, eyes, and nerves after some time. According to the American Heart Association, directing glucose is one of seven estimations for heart health, and these equal estimations make it less slanted to be resolved to have malignancy.

Fatty Intake

The body needs calories for activities and looks after temperature, development, and sufficient body weight. calories are provided mostly via starches and fats. The standard caloric necessity of CKD patients is 35–40 kcal/kg body weight every day. If caloric intake is insufficient, the body uses protein to get calories. This breakdown of protein can prompt severe impacts, for example, lack of healthy sustenance and a more prominent composition of waste items. It is necessary to give a sufficient measure of calories to CKD patients. It is essential to ascertain the caloric necessity indicated by a patient's optimal body weight and not current weight.

Starches

These are the essential source of calories for the body. Starches are in wheat, grains, rice, potatoes, organic products, sugar, nectar, treats, cakes, desserts, and beverages. People with diabetes and fat patients need to confine the measure of starches. It is ideal to use complex sugars from grains like entire wheat and unpolished rice, giving fiber.

These should form a large segment of the sugars in the eating regimen. All other essential sugar-containing substances should not exceed 20% of the total starch consumption, particularly in diabetic patients. Non-diabetic patients may exchange calories from protein with starches as natural products, pies, cakes, treats, jam, or nectar as long as sweets with chocolate, nuts, or bananas are restricted.

Unsaturated or great fats like olive oil, nut oil, canola oil, safflower oil, sunflower oil, fish, and nuts are superior to saturated or terrible fats, for example, red meat, poultry, whole milk, margarine, ghee, cheese, coconut, and grease. Patients with CKD ought to diminish their intake of immersed fats and cholesterol, as these can cause heart disease.

Excessive omega-6 polyunsaturated fats (PUFA) and a too-high omega-6/omega-3 proportion are unsafe, while low omega-6/omega-3 balance applies valuable impacts. Blends of vegetable oil, as opposed to single oil use, will accomplish this reason. Trans fat-containing substances like potato chips, doughnuts, financially arranged treats, and cakes are potentially hurtful and should be avoided.

Limit Protein Intake

Protein is fundamental for the fix and upkeep of body tissues, and it additionally helps in the mending of wounds and battling against disease. Protein confinement (< 0.8 gm/kg body weight/day) is prescribed for CKD patients not on dialysis to diminish the pace of decreased kidney function and defer dialysis and kidney transplantation requirements. Serious protein restriction should be kept away from anyway, given the danger of lack of healthy sustenance. Low craving is normal in CKD patients. Poor hunger and severe protein restriction together can prompt poor nutrition, weight reduction, absence of vitality, and decrease in body opposition, which increment the danger of death. The consumption of protein enhancements and medications, like creatine utilized for muscle advancement, is best kept away except if affirmed by a physician or dietician. Protein intake should be expanded to 1.0–1.2 gm./kg body weight/day to supplant the proteins lost during the methodology when a patient is on dialysis.

Fluid Intake

The kidneys have an essential role in keeping water in the body by expelling excess fluid as urine. As kidney function exacerbates in patients with CKD, the volume of urine generally reduces. Decreased urine yield prompts fluid maintenance in the body, causing puffiness of the face, growing of the legs and hands, and hypertension. The gathering of fluid in the lungs (a condition called pneumonic blockage or edema) causes shortness of breath and trouble relaxing. If this isn't controlled, it tends to be hazardous. Leg growing (edema), ascites (aggregation of fluid in the stomach pit), the brevity of breath, and weight gain in a brief period are the pieces of information that suggest fluid over-burden.

DIFFERENT KIDNEY DISEASES

A severe kidney ailment is the progressive and cumulative decrease of renal function over a long time. In the end, a person will have an irreversible renal illness. Chronic kidney disease, also known as chronic renal disease, is far more common than most people think, and it commonly stays unreported and undetected once the disease has progressed.

When only 25% of a person's renal function is normal, it's not uncommon to discover they have a chronic renal illness. As kidney disease progresses and the organ's function is severely harmed, dangerous levels of waste and fluids will rapidly collect in the body. The purpose of treatment is to stop or limit the progression of the disease, which is usually accomplished by keeping an eye on the cause of the problem.

A Brief Overview of Chronic Renal Disease

There are some issues to consider with chronic renal failure. Blood in the urine, high blood pressure, and tiredness are all common symptoms. The causes are diabetes and a variety of kidney diseases, including polycystic kidney disease. Because there is no cure for chronic renal illness, symptom alleviation is the primary goal of treatment. A blood test, a kidney test, or a biopsy is usually used to make a diagnosis.

The Signs and Symptoms

Persistent kidney disease shows no symptoms until the later stages. However, testing is recommended for people who are at risk. When compared to serious renal failure, chronic renal disease is a slow but steady progression. If one kidney fails, the other may be able to carry on with the normal activity. Signs and consequences usually do not appear until the problem has progressed significantly and the illness has become serious; at this stage, much of the injury is irreversible.

Individuals at a higher risk of developing renal disease should have their renal functions checked regularly, and early detection will considerably lower the risk of serious kidney damage.

The following are the most common symptoms of renal disease:

- Anemia
- Urine with blood
- Pee that is dark in color
- Diminished mental acuity
- Swollen hands, ankles, and feet due to edema (facial if serious edema)
- Tiredness
- High blood pressure (High BP)
- Inability to sleep (insomnia)
- Issues with the skin (may become stubborn)
- Appetite loss.
- Male inability to obtain or maintain an erection (erectile dysfunction).
- More frequent urination, especially at night
- Muscle cramps are a common symptom of menopause.
- Muscular twitches
- Nausea and vomiting
- Pain in the hands or the mid-to-lower back
- Difficulty breathing
- Protein is found in urine.
- Rapid shifts in body weight
- Unexplained aches and pains

While the kidneys perform different tasks, they share a few common diseases. Kidney failure is one such condition caused by genetic mutations, hypertension, and many other factors. This blog post will explore the various diseases which affect the kidneys.

So, what are some of these kidney diseases? Some of them include:

- Acute pyelonephritis

Acute inflammation and infection in both kidneys to cause fever and chills or an infection in one kidney with fever but without evidence of another source of infection.

- Chronic renal failure

A reduction in the kidney function to less than 10% of normal for three months or longer. This will lead to the accumulation of wastes and fluids in the body.

- Nephrotic syndrome

Can be either temporary or permanent and is characterized by an excess in the protein level in the blood plasma and a drop in the protein level within cells. This can lead to kidney failure.

- Polycystic kidney disease

this is a genetic disorder characterized by cysts that can be seen on an ultrasound and are not treatable, and it leads to kidney failure and early death.

- Renal osteodystrophy

This is a malfunctioning of the kidneys, which leads to chronic pain and is usually displayed as pain in the back right below the ribs.

The number of kidney diseases appears to be increasing in the UK, despite a common misconception that the kidneys do not get diseased! Kidney diseases can affect your health in many ways. It can lead to severe complications such as organ failure, loss of body fluids and electrolytes (such as sodium or potassium), and even death.

- Kidney Failure

Kidney failure is a condition where the kidneys cannot adequately filter wastes from the body. Kidneys have an estimated 3 million nephrons, with a small number of blood vessels lining their membranes. When the nephrons fail to do their jobs, wastes and fluids will accumulate from within the body from being flushed out, which will build up fluid and wastes, potentially poison vital organs. This condition can be treated using hemodialysis or a kidney transplant.

IMPORTANCE OF REDUCING THE NUMBER OF PROTEIN FOODS

Dietary control, including protein, phosphorus, and sodium limitation, can impact renal patients by following conventional and nontraditional cardiovascular hazard factors.

Circulatory strain control might be supported by decreasing sodium consumption and the vegan idea of the eating routine, which is significant for bringing down serum cholesterol and improving the plasma lipid profile.

Protein-limited eating regimens may likewise have to calm and against oxidant properties.

The general principles of diet treatment for chronic kidney patients are as follows:

- Limit protein intake to 0.8 gm/kg per kilogram per day for non-dialysis patients. Patients on dialysis need a greater amount of protein to compensate for the possible loss of proteins during the procedure. (1.0 to 1.2 gm/kg daily according to body weight)
- Take enough carbohydrates to provide energy
- Take average amounts of oil—reduction of butter, pure fat, and oil intake.
- Restriction of fluid and water intake in case of swelling (edema)
- Dietary intake of sodium, potassium, and phosphorus limitation
- Take adequate amounts of vitamins and trace elements. A high-fiber diet is recommended.

The details of the selection and modification of the diet for chronic kidney patients are as follows:

High-Calorie Intake

In addition to daily activities to maintain heat, growth, and body weight, the body needs calories. Calories are taken with carbohydrates and fats. According to body weight, the daily regular calorie intake of patients suffering from chronic kidney disease is 35-40 kcal/kg. If caloric intake is insufficient, the body uses proteins to provide calories. Such protein distribution may cause harmful effects, such as improper nutrition and increased production of waste materials. Therefore, it is essential to provide sufficient calories to CKD patients. It is important to calculate the patient's daily calorie requirement based on the ideal body weight, not the current weight.

Carbohydrates

Carbohydrates are the primary source of calories required for the body. Diabetes and obesity patients should limit the number of carbohydrates. It is best to use complex carbohydrates obtained from whole grains such as whole wheat or raw rice that can provide fiber. They should constitute a large part of the number of carbohydrates in the diet. The proportion of all other sugar-containing substances should not exceed 20% of the total carbohydrate intake, particularly in diabetic patients. As long as chocolate, hazelnut, or banana desserts are consumed in a limited amount, non-diabetic patients may be replaced with calories, fruit, pies, pastry, cookies, and protein.

Oils

Fats are a source of calories for the body and provide twice as many carbohydrates and proteins. Chronic kidney patients should limit the intake of saturated fat and cholesterol that may cause heart disease. In unsaturated fat, it is necessary to pay attention to the proportion of monounsaturated fat and polyunsaturated fat. Excessive uptake of omega-6 polyunsaturated fatty acids (CFAs) and a relatively high omega-6/omega-3 ratio are detrimental, while the low omega-6/omega-3 ratio has beneficial effects. The use of vegetable oils instead of uniform oils will achieve this goal. Trans fat-containing substances such as potato chips, sweet buns, instant cookies, and pastries are extremely dangerous and should be avoided.

Restriction of Protein Intake

Protein is essential for the restoration and maintenance of body tissues, and it also helps heal wounds and fight infection. In patients with chronic renal failure who do not undergo dialysis, protein limitation is recommended to reduce the decrease in renal function and postpone the need for dialysis and renal transplantation. (<0.8 gm/kg daily according to body weight). However, excessive protein restriction should also be avoided due to the risk of malnutrition.

Anorexia is a common condition in patients with chronic kidney disease. Strict protein restriction, poor diet, weight loss, fatigue, loss of body resistance, and loss of appetite increase the risk of death. High proteins such as meat, poultry, and fish, eggs, and tofu are preferred. Chronic kidney patients should avoid high protein diets. Similarly, protein supplements or medications such as creatinine used for muscle development should be avoided unless recommended by a physician or dietician. However, as the patient begins dialysis, daily protein intake should be increased by 1.0 to 1.2 gm/kg body weight to recover the proteins lost during the procedure.

Fluid intake

Why should chronic kidney patients take precautions about fluid intake?

The kidneys are important in maintaining the correct amount of water by removing excess liquid as urea. In patients with chronic kidney disease, the urea volume usually decreases as the kidney functions deteriorate. Reduction of urea excretion from the body causes fluid retention, resulting in facial swelling, swelling of legs and hands, and high blood pressure. A build-up of fluid in the lungs causes shortness of breath and difficulty breathing. It can be life-threatening if not checked.

What precautions should chronic kidney patients take to control fluid intake?

The amount of fluid taken on a physician's advice should be recorded and monitored to prevent overloading or loss of fluid. The amount of water to be taken for each chronic kidney patient may vary, and this rate is calculated according to each patient's urea excretion and fluid status.

What is the recommended amount of fluid for patients with chronic kidney disease?

Unlimited edema and water intake can be done in patients with edema and can throw enough urea from the body. It is a common mistake that patients with kidney disease should take large amounts of water and fluids to protect their kidneys. The recommended amount of liquid depends on the patient's clinical condition and renal function.

Patients with edema who cannot appoint sufficient urea from the body should limit fluid intake. To reduce swelling, fluid intake within 24 hours should be less than the amount of urine produced by the daily body.

In patients with edema, the amount of fluid taken daily should be 500 ml more than the previous day's urine volume to prevent fluid overload or fluid loss. This additional 500 ml of liquid will approximately compensate for the fluids lost by perspiration and exhalation.

Why should chronic kidney patients keep a record of their daily weight?

Patients need to record their weight daily to detect fluid increase or loss or to monitor fluid volume in their bodies. Bodyweight will remain constant if the instructions for fluid intake are strictly followed. Sudden weight gain indicates excessive fluid overload due to increased fluid intake in the body, and weight gain is a warning that the patient should make more rigorous fluid restrictions. Weight loss is usually caused by fluid restriction and the use of diuretics.

Useful Tips for Restricting Fluid Intake

Reduce salty, spicy, or fried foods in your diet because these foods can increase your thirst and cause more fluid consumption.

Only drink water when you are thirsty. Avoid drinking as a habit or because everyone drinks

When thirsty, consume only a small amount of water or try ice — sure, taking a little ice cube. Ice stays in the mouth longer than water to give a more satisfying result than the same amount of water. Remember to calculate the amount of liquid consumed. To calculate, freeze the amount of water allocated for drinking in the ice block.

To prevent dry mouth, gargle with water, but do not swallow the water. Dry mouth can also be reduced by chewing gum, sucking hard candies, lemon slices, or mint candies, and using a small amount of water to moisturize your mouth.

Always use small cups or glasses to limit fluid intake. Instead of consuming extra water for medication use, take your medicines while drinking water after meals.

High blood sugar in diabetic patients can increase the level of thirst. It is essential to keep blood sugar under tight control to reduce thirst.

Since the person's thirst increases in hot weather, measures to be in cooler environments may be preferred and recommended.

D uring kidney disease, this is extremely important. They can advise you about the favorite foods' sodium, phosphorous, and potassium content and recommend reducing your sodium intake. Your diet will be tailored to you, considering the stage of kidney disease you're in and any other illnesses or diseases you suffer from.

Keep a Food Diary

You should track what you're eating and drinking to stay within the guidelines and recommendations given to you. Apps such as My Fitness Pal make this extremely easy and even track many minerals and levels in foods, including sodium, protein, etc. There are also apps specifically made for kidney disease patients to track sodium, phosphorous, and potassium levels.

Read Food Labels

Some foods have hidden sodium in them, even if they don't taste salty. You will need to cut back on the amount of canned, frozen, and processed foods you eat. Check your beverages for added sodium.

Check food labels to avoid

Potassium chloride, Tetrasodium phosphate, Sodium phosphate, Trisodium phosphate, Tricalcium phosphate, Phosphoric acid, Polyphosphate, Hexametaphosphate, Pyrophosphate, Monocalcium phosphate, Dicalcium phosphate, Aluminum phosphate, Sodium tripolyphosphate, Sodium polyphosphate.

Flavor foods with spices and herbs rather than shop-bought dressings and condiments

These add flavor and variety to your meals and are not packed with sodium; spices also have many health benefits. Stay away from salt substitutes and seasonings that contain potassium. Use citrus fruits and vinegar for dressings and to add flavor.

Keep up your appointments with your Doctor or Nephrologist

Let your doctor know if you notice any swelling or changes in your weight.

Monitor drink and fluid intake

You have likely been told you need to drink up to eight glasses of water a day. This is true for a healthy body, but for people experiencing the later stages of CKD, these fluids can build up and cause additional problems. The restriction of fluids will differ from person to person. Things to take into consideration are swelling urine output and weight gain. Your weight will be recorded before dialysis begins and once it's over. This is done to determine how much fluid to remove from your body. If you are undergoing hemodialysis, this will be recorded approximately three times a week. If you are undergoing peritoneal dialysis, your weight is recorded every day. If there is a significant weight gain, you may be drinking too much fluids.

Measure portion sizes

Moderating your portion sizes is essential. Use smaller cups, bowls, or plates to avoid giving yourself oversized portions.

Measure your food so you can keep an accurate record of how much you are eating:

- The size of a fist is equal to 1 cup.
- The palm is equal to 3 oz.
- The tip of your thumb is equivalent to 1 tsp.
- A poker chip is equal to 1 tbsp.

Substitution Tips

- Use plain white flour instead of whole-wheat/whole grain

- Use all-purpose flour instead of self-raising,
- Use Stevia instead of sugar,
- Use egg whites rather than whole eggs,
- Use soy milk or almond rice instead of cow's milk.

Other Advice

- Be careful when eating in restaurants—ask for dressings and condiments on the side and watch out for soups and cured meats.
- Watch out for convenience foods that are high in sodium.
- Prepare your meals and freeze them for future use.
- Drain liquids from canned vegetables and fruits to help control potassium levels.

FOODS TO AVOID AND WHAT TO EAT

Food to Eat

The renal diet aims to cut down the amount of waste in the blood. When people have kidney dysfunction, the kidneys are unable to remove and filter waste properly. When waste is left in the blood, it can affect the electrolyte levels of the patient. With a kidney diet, kidney function is promoted, and the progression of complete kidney failure is slowed down.

The renal diet follows a low intake of protein, phosphorus, and sodium. It is necessary to consume high-quality protein and limit some fluids. For some people, it is important to limit calcium and potassium.

Promoting a renal diet, here are the substances which are critical to be monitored:

Sodium and its role in the body

Most natural foods contain sodium. Some people think that sodium and salt are interchangeable, and however, salt is a comb of chloride and sodium. There might be either salt or sodium in other forms in the food we eat. Due to the added salt, processed foods include a higher level of sodium.

Apart from potassium and chloride, sodium is one of the most crucial body's electrolytes. The main function of electrolytes is to control the fluids when they are going out and in the body's cells and tissues.

With sodium:

- Blood volume and pressure are regulated.
- Muscle contraction and nerve function are regulated.
- The acid-base balance of the blood is monitored.
- The amount of fluid the body eliminates and keeps is balanced.

Why is it important to monitor sodium intake for people with kidney issues?

Since the kidneys of kidney disease patients cannot reduce excess fluid and sodium from the body adequately, too much sodium might be harmful. As fluid and sodium build up in the bloodstream and tissues, they might cause:

- Edema: swelling in face, hands, and legs.
- Increased thirst.
- High blood pressure.
- Shortness of breath.
- Heart failure.

The ways to monitor sodium intake:

- Avoid processed foods.
- Be attentive to serving sizes.
- Read food labels.
- Utilize fresh meats instead of processed.
- Choose fresh fruits and veggies.
- Compare brands, choosing the ones with the lowest sodium levels.
- Utilize spices that do not include salt.
- Ensure the sodium content is less than 400 mg per meal and not more than 150 mg per snack.
- Cook at home, not adding salt.

Foods to eat with lower sodium content:

- Fresh meats, dairy products, frozen veggies, and fruits.
- Fresh herbs and seasonings like rosemary, oregano, dill, lime, cilantro, onion, lemon, and garlic.
- Corn tortilla chips, pretzels, no salt added crackers, unsalted popcorn.

Potassium and its role in the body

The main function of potassium is keeping muscles working correctly and the heartbeat regular. This mineral is responsible for maintaining electrolyte and fluid balance in the bloodstream. The kidneys regulate the proper amount of potassium in the body, expelling excess amounts in the urine.

Monitoring potassium intake

- Limit high potassium food.
- Select only fresh fruits and veggies.
- Limit dairy products and milk to 8 oz. per day.
- Avoid potassium chloride.
- Read labels on packaged foods.
- Avoid seasonings and salt substitutes with potassium.

Foods to eat with lower potassium:

- Fruits: watermelon, tangerines, pineapple, plums, peaches, pears, papayas, mangoes, lemons and limes, honeydew, grapefruit/grapefruit juice, grapes/grape juice, clementine/satsuma, cranberry juice, berries, and apples/applesauce, apple juice.
- Veggies: summer squash (cooked), okra, mushrooms (fresh), lettuce, kale, green beans, eggplant, cucumber, corn, onions (raw), celery, cauliflower, carrots, cabbage, broccoli (fresh), bamboo shoots (canned), and bell peppers.
- Plain Turkish delights, marshmallows and jellies, boiled fruit sweets, and peppermints.
- Shortbread, ginger nut biscuits, plain digestives.
- Plain flapjacks and cereal bars.
- Plain sponge cakes like Madeira cake, lemon sponge, jam sponge.
- Corn-based and wheat crisps.
- Whole grain crispbreads and crackers.
- Protein and other foods (bread (not whole grain), pasta, noodles, rice, eggs, canned tuna, turkey (white meat), and chicken (white meat).

Phosphorus and its role in the body

This mineral is essential in bone development and maintenance. Phosphorus helps in the development of connective organs and tissue and assists in muscle movement. Extra phosphorus is possible to be removed by healthy kidneys. However, it is impossible with kidney dysfunction. High levels of phosphorus make weak bones by pulling calcium out of your bones, and it might lead to dangerous calcium deposits in the heart, eyes, lungs, and blood vessels.

Monitoring phosphorus intake

- Pay attention to serving size.
- Eat fresh fruits and veggies.
- Eat smaller portions of foods that are rich in protein.
- Avoid packaged foods.
- Keep a food journal.

Foods to eat with low phosphorus levels:

- Grapes, apples.
- Lettuce, leeks.
- Carbohydrates (white rice, corn, and rice Cereal, popcorn, pasta, crackers (not wheat), white bread)
- Meat (sausage, fresh meat).

Protein

Damaged kidneys are unable to remove protein waste, so they accumulate in the blood. The amount of protein to consume differs depending on the stage of CKD. Protein is critical for tissue maintenance, and it is necessary to eat the proper amount of it according to the particular stage of kidneys disease.

Sources of protein for vegetarians:

- Vegans (allowing only plant-based foods): Wheat protein and whole grains, nut butter, soy protein, yogurt, or soy milk, cooked no salt added canned and dried beans and peas, unsalted nuts.
- Lacto vegetarians (allowing dairy products, milk, and plant-based foods): reduced-sodium or low-sodium cottage cheese.
- Lacto-Ovo vegetarians (allowing eggs, dairy products, milk, and plant-based foods): eggs.

Food to Avoid

Food with high sodium content

- Onion salt, marinades, garlic salt, teriyaki sauce, and table salt.
- Pepperoni, bacon, ham, lunch meat, hot dogs, sausage, processed meats.
- Ramen noodles, canned produce, and canned soups.
- Marinara sauce, gravy, salad dressings, soy sauce, BBQ sauce, and ketchup.
- Chex Mix, salted nuts, Cheetos, crackers, and potato chips.
- Fast food.

Food with a high potassium level

- Fruits: dried fruit, oranges/orange juice, prunes/prune juice, kiwi, nectarines, dates, cantaloupe, bananas, black currants, damsons, cherries, grapes, and apricots.
- Vegetables: tomatoes/tomato sauce/tomato juice, sweet potatoes, beans, lentils, split peas, spinach (cooked), pumpkin, potatoes, mushrooms (cooked), chile peppers, chard, Brussels sprouts (cooked), broccoli (cooked), baked beans, avocado, butternut squash, and acorn squash.
- Protein and other foods: peanut butter, molasses, granola, chocolate, bran, sardines, fish, bacon, ham, nuts and seeds, yogurt, milkshakes, and milk.
- Coconut-based snacks, nut-based snacks, fudge, and toffee.
- Cakes contain marzipan.
- Potato crisps.

Foods with high phosphorus

- Dairy products: pudding, ice cream, yogurt, cottage cheese, cheese, and milk.
- Nuts and seeds: sunflower seeds, pumpkin seeds, pecans, peanut butter, pistachios, cashews, and almonds.
- Dried beans and peas: soybeans, split peas, refried beans, pinto beans, lentils, kidney beans, garbanzo beans, black beans, and baked beans.
- Meat: veal, turkey, liver, lamb, beef, bacon, fish, and seafood.
- Carbohydrates: whole grain products, oatmeal, and bran cereals.

Renal Diet Shopping List

Vegetables

- Arugula (raw)
- Alfalfa sprouts
- Bamboo shoots
- Asparagus
- Beans—pinto, wax, fava, green
- Bean sprouts
- Bitter melon (balsam pear)
- Beet greens (raw)
- Broccoli
- Broad beans (boiled, fresh)
- Cactus
- Cabbage—red, swamp, Napa/Suey Choy, skunk
- Carrots
- Calabash
- Celery
- Cauliflower
- Chayote
- Celeriac (cooked)
- Collard greens
- Chicory
- Cucumber
- Corn
- Okra
- Onions
- Pepitas
- (Green) Peas
- Peppers
- Radish
- Radicchio
- Seaweed
- Rapini (raw)
- Shallots
- Spinach (raw)
- Snow peas
- Dandelion greens (raw)
- Daikon
- Plant Leaves
- Drumstick
- Endive
- Eggplant
- Fennel bulb.
- Escarole
- Fiddlehead greens
- Ferns
- Hearts of Palm

- Irish moss
- Hominy
- Jicama, raw
- Leeks
- Kale(raw)
- Mushrooms (raw white)
- Lettuce (raw)
- Mustard greens
- Swiss chard (raw)
- Squash
- Turnip
- Tomatillos (raw)
- Watercress
- Turnip greens
- Wax beans
- Water chestnuts (canned)
- Winter melon
- Wax gourd
- Zucchini (raw)

Fruits

- Acerola Cherries
- Apple
- Blackberries
- Asian Pear
- Boysenberries
- Blueberries
- Cherries
- Casaba melon
- Clementine
- Chokeberries
- Crabapples
- Cloudberries
- Cranberries (fresh)
- Grapefruit
- Gooseberries
- Pomegranate
- Grapes
- Rambutan
- Quince
- Rhubarb
- Raspberries (fresh or frozen)
- Jujubes
- Golden Berry
- Kumquat
- Jackfruit
- Lingonberries
- Lemon

- Loganberries
- Lime
- Lychees
- Mango
- Mandarin orange
- Peach
- Pineapple
- Pear
- Plum
- Strawberries
- Rose-apple
- Tangerine
- Tangelo
- Watermelon

Fresh Meat, Seafood, and Poultry

- Chicken
- Beef and Ground Beef
- Goat
- Duck
- Wild Game
- Pork
- Lamb
- Veal
- Turkey
- Fish

Milk, Eggs, and Dairy

Milk:

- Milk (½-1 cup/day)

Non-Dairy Milk:

- Almond Fresh (Original, Unsweetened, Vanilla).
- Almond Breeze (Original, Vanilla, Vanilla Unsweetened, Original Unsweetened).
- Silk True Almond Beverage (Unsweetened Original, Original, Vanilla, Unsweetened Vanilla).
- Good Karma Flax Delight (Vanilla, Original, Unsweetened).
- Rice Dream Rice Drink (Vanilla Classic, Non-Enriched Original Classic).
- Silk Soy Beverage (Original, Vanilla, Unsweetened).
- Natura Organic Fortified Rice Beverage (Original, Vanilla).
- PC Organics Fortified Rice Beverage.

Other Dairy Products:

- Non-Hydrogenated Margarine (Salt-Free or Regular).
- Butter (Unsalted or Regular).
- Whipping Cream.
- Sour Cream.
- Whipped Cream.

RENAL DIET IN 4 SEASONS OF THE YEAR

This provides a summary of how to eat a healthy diet during different times of the year. It includes the four seasons and shows the foods you should and not be eating in each season.

Spring

Introduce more fluids and fiber to the diet. Reduce concentrated carbohydrate intake but increase protein intake to help rebuild tissues damaged by treatment. Encourage high-fiber foods (vegetables, fruits, grains). Fruits and vegetables have high water content in them. This makes them a safe and low-calorie choice in a restricted diet.

Summer

Consume fluids and fruits that are high in potassium content. Potassium is important for maintaining healthy blood pressure levels and preventing heart rhythm abnormalities. Vegetables are also allowed but in moderation with high salt content to avoid fluid retention in the body.

Fall

Fruits should be eaten in moderation. Protein-rich foods (meat, fish, beans) should be eaten in moderation or avoided altogether. Instead, increase fruit and vegetable intake; emphasize vegetables with cooling properties (onions, garlic, Brussels sprouts). Add legumes (beans, lentils, chickpeas) to the diet.

Winter

Keep a balance of carbohydrates and proteins. Reduce fat intake by limiting beef and lamb to no more than twice a week but include fish and eggs or dairy products to increase fat intake from other sources such as whole-grain bread and cereals that contain good fats.

Spring	Summer	Fall	Winter
What to eat:	What to eat:	What to eat:	What to eat:
• Vegetables, especially fruits and grains • Fresh fruits are great sources of fluid, potassium, magnesium, B vitamins, phosphorus, zinc	• Fruits: apples, strawberries, kiwi fruits • Vegetables: lettuce, celery, cucumber, lettuce • Root crops: carrots, sweet potatoes, rutabaga, beets • Legumes: kidney beans, black-eyed peas, lentils • Leaner cuts of meat: pork, chicken breast • Eggs • Dairy: raw milk, yogurt, goat's milk.	• Fruits: bananas, apples, pears, grapes • Vegetables: lettuce, celery, onions, celery root • Legumes: green peas, lentils • Lean meats: turkey • Tofu • Eggs	• Vegetables: Chinese cabbage, spinach, lettuce, kale • Fruits: apples, oranges • Legumes: soybeans • Lean meats: lean fish cuts of beef and lamb • Eggs

What to Avoid:	What to Avoid:	What to Avoid:	What to Avoid:
• Fatty foods that are high in cholesterol and saturated fat • Decrease intake of refined carbohydrate (bread), high sugar food (candy) • High protein food should be kept to a minimum	• Sugary foods: candies, pastries • Fruit juice or any sweet drink • High-fat meats: pork, beef, ham, bacon • Fried foods: French fries, fried chicken. • Baked foods: cookies, cakes, whipped cream. • Sugar cane	• Fatty meats: pork, bacon • Sugary foods: cakes, cookies, pastries • Added salt in food • Dairy: cheese, cream • Sugary foods: candies, pastries	• Fatty meats: beef, lamb, pork • Skin or organ of animals (including butter) or eggs • High-sodium foods: canned soup; salt; relishes; processed food (e.g., breads and cereals); snacks such as chips and pretzels • Alcohol

BREAKFAST RECIPES

1. Turkey and Spinach Scramble on Melba Toast

Preparation Time: 5 minutes
Cooking Time: 15 minutes
Servings: 2
INGREDIENTS:

- 1 tsp. extra virgin olive oil
- 1 cup raw spinach
- ½ garlic clove, minced
- 1 tsp. nutmeg, grated
- 1 cup turkey breast, cooked and diced
- 4 slices melba toast
- 1 tsp. balsamic vinegar

DIRECTIONS:
1. Prepare a skillet over medium heat, then add oil.
2. Add turkey and heat through for 6 to 8 minutes.
3. Add spinach, garlic, and nutmeg and stir-fry for 6 minutes more.
4. Plate up the Melba toast and top with spinach and turkey scramble.
5. Drizzle with balsamic vinegar and serve.

NUTRITION:

- Calories: 301 kcal
- Fat: 19 g
- Carb: 12 g
- Protein: 19 g
- Sodium: 360 mg
- Potassium: 269 mg
- Phosphorus: 215 mg

2. Cheesy Scrambled Eggs with Fresh Herbs

Preparation Time: 15 minutes
Cooking Time: 10 minutes
Servings: 4
INGREDIENTS:

- 3 eggs
- 2 egg whites
- ½ cup cream cheese
- ¼ cup rice milk, unsweetened
- 1 tbsp. green part only scallion, chopped
- 1 tbsp. fresh tarragon, chopped
- 2 tbsp. butter, unsalted
- Black pepper, ground, to taste

DIRECTIONS:
1. Whisk the eggs, egg whites, cream cheese, rice milk, scallions, and tarragon. Mix until smooth.
2. Melt the butter in a skillet.
3. Put egg mixture and cook for 5 minutes or until the eggs are thick and curds creamy.
4. Season with pepper and serve.

NUTRITION:

- Calories: 221 kcal
- Fat: 19 g
- Carb: 3 g
- Protein: 8 g
- Sodium: 193 mg
- Potassium: 140 mg
- Phosphorus: 119 mg

3. Bulgur, Couscous, and Buckwheat Cereal

Preparation Time: 10 minutes
Cooking Time: 25 minutes
Servings: 4
INGREDIENTS:

- 2 ¼ cups water
- 1 ¼ cups vanilla rice milk
- 6 tbsp. bulgur, uncooked
- 2 tbsp. whole buckwheat, uncooked
- 1 cup apple, sliced
- 6 tbsp. plain couscous, uncooked
- ½ tsp. cinnamon, ground

DIRECTIONS:
1. Heat the water and milk in the saucepan over medium heat. Let it boil.
2. Put the bulgur, buckwheat, and apple.
3. Lower heat and simmer, occasionally stirring until the bulgur is tender, about 20 to 25 minutes.
4. Remove the saucepan and stir in the couscous and cinnamon—cover for 10 minutes.
5. Put the cereal before serving.

NUTRITION:

- Calories: 159 kcal
- Fat: 1 g
- Carb: 34 g
- Protein: 4 g
- Sodium: 33 mg
- Potassium: 116 mg
- Phosphorus: 130 mg

4. Blueberry Muffins

Preparation Time: 15 minutes
Cooking Time: 30 minutes
Servings: 12
INGREDIENTS:

- 2 cups rice milk, unsweetened
- 1 tbsp. apple cider vinegar
- 3 ½ cups all-purpose flour
- 1 cup sugar, granulated
- 1 tbsp. baking soda substitute
- 1 tsp. cinnamon, ground
- ½ tsp. nutmeg, ground
- A pinch ginger, ground
- ½ cup canola oil
- 2 tbsp. pure vanilla extract
- 2 ½ cups fresh blueberries

DIRECTIONS:
1. Preheat the oven to 375°F.
2. Prepare a muffin pan and set it aside.
3. Stir together the rice milk and vinegar in a small bowl. Set aside for 10 minutes.
4. Stir the sugar, flour, baking soda, cinnamon, nutmeg, and ginger in a large bowl, until well mixed.
5. Add oil and vanilla to the milk and mix.
6. Put milk mixture to dry ingredients and stir well to combine.
7. Put the blueberries and spoon the muffin batter evenly into the cups.
8. Bake the muffins for 25 to 30 minutes or until golden and a toothpick inserted comes out clean.
9. Cool for 15 minutes and serve.

NUTRITION:

- Calories: 331 kcal
- Fat: 11 g
- Carb: 52 g
- Protein: 6 g
- Sodium: 35 mg
- Potassium: 89 mg
- Phosphorus: 90 mg

5. Buckwheat and Grapefruit Porridge

Preparation Time: 5 minutes
Cooking Time: 20 minutes
Servings: 2
INGREDIENTS:

- ½ cup buckwheat
- ¼ grapefruit, chopped
- 1 tbsp. honey
- 1 ½ cups almond milk
- 2 cups water

DIRECTIONS:
1. Let the water boil on the stove. Add the buckwheat and place the lid on the pan.
2. Lower heat slightly and simmer for 7 to 10 minutes, checking to ensure water does not dry out.

3. When most of the water is absorbed, remove, and set aside for 5 minutes.
4. Drain any excess water from the pan and stir in almond milk, heating through for 5 minutes.
5. Add the honey and grapefruit.
6. Serve.

NUTRITION:

- Calories: 231 kcal
- Fat: 4 g
- Carb: 43 g
- Protein: 13 g
- Sodium: 135 mg
- Potassium: 370 mg
- Phosphorus: 165 mg

6. Egg and Veggie Muffins

Preparation Time: 15 minutes
Cooking Time: 20 minutes
Servings: 4
INGREDIENTS:

- 4 eggs
- 2 tbsp. rice milk, unsweetened
- ½ sweet onion, chopped
- ½ red bell pepper, chopped
- A pinch black pepper, ground
- A pinch red pepper flakes

DIRECTIONS:
1. Preheat the oven to 350°F.
2. Spray oil in the 4 muffin pans. Put aside.
3. Prepare the milk, eggs, onion, red pepper, parsley, red pepper flakes, and black pepper. Whisk until mixed.
4. Gently put the egg mixture into muffin pans.
5. Bake for about 18 to 20 minutes or until the muffins are puffed and golden.
6. Serve.

NUTRITION:

- Calories: 84 kcal
- Fat: 5 g
- Carb: 3 g
- Protein: 7 g
- Sodium: 75 mg
- Potassium: 117 mg
- Phosphorus: 110 mg

7. Berry Chia with Yogurt

Preparation Time: 35 minutes
Cooking Time: 5 minutes
Servings: 4

INGREDIENTS:

- ½ cup chia seeds, dried
- 2 cups yogurt (plain)
- ⅓ cup strawberries, chopped
- 4 tsp. Splenda
- ¼ cup blackberries
- ¼ cup raspberries

DIRECTIONS:
1. Put together the plain yogurt with Splenda and chia seeds.
2. Move the mixture into the serving ramekins and leave it for 35 minutes.
3. Add raspberries, strawberries, and blackberries. Mix well.
4. Serve it immediately or keep it in the fridge up to 2 days.

NUTRITION:

- Calories: 150 kcal
- Fat: 5 g
- Carbs: 19 g
- Protein: 6.8 g
- Sodium: 65 mg
- Potassium: 226 mg
- Phosphorus: 75 mg

8. Arugula Eggs with Chili Peppers

Preparation Time: 7 minutes
Cooking Time: 10 minutes
Servings: 4
INGREDIENTS:

- 2 cups arugula, chopped
- 3 eggs, beaten
- ½ chili pepper, chopped
- 1 tbsp. butter
- 1 oz. Parmesan, grated

DIRECTIONS:
1. Toss butter in the skillet and melt it.
2. Add arugula and sauté it over medium heat for 5 minutes. Stir it from time to time.
3. Meanwhile, mix up together Parmesan, chili pepper, and eggs.
4. Pour the egg mixture over the arugula and scramble well.
5. Cook for 5 minutes more over medium heat.

NUTRITION:

- Calories: 218 kcal
- Fat: 15 g
- Carbs: 2.8 g
- Protein: 17 g
- Sodium: 656 mg
- Potassium: 243 mg
- Phosphorus: 310 mg

9. Eggplant Chicken Sandwich

Preparation Time: 10 minutes
Cooking Time: 15 minutes
Servings: 2
INGREDIENTS:

- 1 eggplant, trimmed
- 10 oz. chicken fillet
- 1 tsp. Plain yogurt
- ½ tsp. garlic, minced
- 1 tbsp. fresh cilantro, chopped
- 2 lettuce leaves
- 1 tsp. olive oil
- ½ tsp. salt
- ½ tsp. chili pepper
- 1 tsp. butter

DIRECTIONS:

1. Slice the eggplant lengthwise into 4 slices.
2. Rub the eggplant slices with minced garlic and brush with olive oil.
3. Grill the eggplant slices on the preheated to 375°F grill for 3 minutes from each side.
4. Meanwhile, rub the chicken fillet with salt and chili pepper.
5. Place it in the skillet and add butter.
6. Roast the chicken for 6 minutes from each side over medium-high heat.
7. Cool the cooked eggplants gently and spread one side of them with Plain yogurt.
8. Add lettuce leaves and chopped fresh cilantro.
9. After this, slice the cooked chicken fillet and add over the lettuce.
10. Cover it with the remaining sliced eggplant to get the sandwich shape. Pin the sandwich with the toothpick if needed.

NUTRITION:

- Calories: 276 kcal
- Fat: 11 g
- Carbs: 41 g
- Protein: 13.8 g
- Sodium: 775 mg
- Potassium: 532 mg
- Phosphorus: 187 mg

10. Eggs in Tomato Rings

Preparation Time: 8 minutes
Cooking Time: 5 minutes
Servings: 2
INGREDIENTS:

- 1 tomato
- 2 eggs
- ¼ tsp. chili flakes
- ¾ tsp. salt
- ½ tsp. butter

DIRECTIONS:

1. Trim the tomato and slice it into 2 rings.
2. Remove the tomato flesh.
3. Toss butter in the skillet and melt it.
4. Then arrange the tomato rings.
5. Crack the eggs in the tomato rings. Sprinkle them with salt and chili flakes.
6. Cook the eggs for 4 minutes over medium heat with the closed lid.
7. Transfer the cooked eggs to the serving plates with the help of the spatula.

NUTRITION:

- Calories: 237 kcal
- Fat: 16 g
- Carbs: 7 g
- Protein: 16 g
- Sodium: 427 mg
- Potassium: 391.5 mg
- Phosphorus: 291 mg

11. Chorizo Bowl with Corn

Preparation Time: 10 minutes
Cooking Time: 15 minutes
Servings: 4
INGREDIENTS:

- 9 oz. chorizo
- 1 tbsp. almond butter
- ½ cup corn kernels
- 1 tomato, chopped
- ¾ cup heavy cream
- 1 tsp. butter

- ¼ tsp. chili pepper
- 1 tbsp. dill, chopped

DIRECTIONS:
1. Cut the chorizo and place it in the skillet.
2. Add almond butter and chili pepper.
3. Roast the chorizo for 3 minutes.
4. After this, add tomato and corn kernels.
5. Put the butter and cut the dill. Stir up the mixture well.
6. Cook for 2 minutes.
7. Simmer with the closed lid for 10 minutes.
8. Move into the serving bowls.

NUTRITION:

- Calories: 286 kcal
- Fat: 15 g
- Carbs: 26 g
- Protein: 13 g
- Sodium: 228 mg
- Potassium: 255 mg
- Phosphorus: 293 mg

12. Panzanella Salad

Preparation Time: 10 minutes
Cooking Time: 5 minutes
Servings: 4
INGREDIENTS:

- 3 tomatoes, chopped
- 2 cucumbers, chopped
- 1 red onion, sliced
- 2 red bell peppers, chopped
- ¼ cup fresh cilantro, chopped
- 1 tbsp. capers
- 1 oz. whole-grain bread, chopped
- 1 tbsp. canola oil
- ½ tsp. garlic, minced
- 1 tbsp. Dijon mustard
- 1 tsp. olive oil
- 1 tsp. lime juice

DIRECTIONS:
1. Add oil into the skillet and let it to boil.
2. Add sliced bread and toast for 5 minutes until crunchy.
3. In the salad bowl, put the sliced red onion, cucumbers, tomatoes, bell peppers, cilantro, capers, and mix up gently.
4. Make the dressing: mix up olive oil, lime juice, minced garlic, and Dijon mustard.
5. Add the dressing over the salad and stir it directly before serving.

NUTRITION:

- Calories: 224.3 kcal

- Fat: 10 g
- Carbs: 26 g
- Protein: 6.6 g
- Sodium: 401 mg
- Potassium: 324.9 mg
- Phosphorus: 84 mg

13. Poached Egg with Asparagus

Preparation Time: 3 minutes
Cooking Time: 15 minutes
Servings: 1
INGREDIENTS:

- 4 spears asparagus
- 1 egg
- Water

DIRECTIONS:
1. Put half deep water in the saucepan and set over high heat. Let it boil.
2. Soak asparagus in the water. Cook until turn into a shade brighter, about 3 minutes.
3. Remove from saucepan and drain on paper towels. Keep warm—lightly season before serving.
4. Use a slotted spoon to lower the egg into boiling water gently.
5. Cook for only 4 minutes. Remove from pan immediately. Place on egg holder.
6. Slice off the top. The egg should still be fluid inside.
7. Place asparagus spears on a small plate and serve egg on the side.
8. Dip asparagus into the egg and eat while warm.

NUTRITION:

- Calories: 178 kcal
- Fat: 13 g
- Carbs: 1 g
- Protein: 7.72 g
- Sodium: 71 mg
- Potassium: 203 mg
- Phosphorus: 124 mg

14. Egg Drop Soup

Preparation Time: 5 minutes
Cooking Time: 10 minutes
Servings: 4
INGREDIENTS:

- ¼ cup fresh chives, minced
- 4 cups vegetable stock, unsalted
- 4 eggs, whisked

DIRECTIONS:
1. Pour unsalted vegetable stock into the oven set over high heat. Bring to a boil. Lower heat.
2. Pour in the eggs. Stir until ribbons form into the soup.
3. Turn off the heat immediately. The residual heat will cook eggs through.
4. Cool slightly before ladling the desired amount into individual bowls. Garnish with a pinch of parsley, if using.
5. Serve immediately.

NUTRITION:

- Calories: 73 kcal
- Fat: 3 g
- Carbs: 1 g
- Protein: 7 g
- Sodium: 891 mg
- Potassium: 53 mg
- Phosphorus: 36 mg

15. Raspberry Overnight Porridge

Preparation Time: 5 minutes
Cooking Time: Overnight
Servings: 1
INGREDIENTS:

- ⅓ cup oats rolled
- ½ cup almond milk
- 1 tbsp. honey
- 5–6 raspberries, fresh or canned, and unsweetened

DIRECTIONS:
1. Combine the oats, almond milk, and honey in a mason jar and place it into the fridge overnight.
2. Serve the following morning with the raspberries on top.

NUTRITION:

- Calories: 143.6 kcal
- Fat: 3.91 g
- Carbohydrate: 34.62 g
- Protein: 3.44 g
- Sodium: 77.88 mg
- Potassium: 153.25 mg
- Phosphorus: 99.3 mg

16. Summer Veggie Omelet

Preparation Time: 5 minutes
Cooking Time: 5 minutes
Servings: 2
INGREDIENTS:

- 4 large egg whites
- ¼ cup sweet corn, frozen
- ⅓ cup zucchini, grated
- 2 green onions, sliced
- 1 tbsp. cream cheese
- Kosher pepper

DIRECTIONS:
1. Grease a medium pan with some cooking spray and add the onions, corn, and grated zucchini.
2. Sauté for a couple of minutes until softened.
3. Beat the eggs together with the water, cream cheese, and pepper in a bowl.
4. Add the eggs into the veggie mixture in the pan and let cook while moving the edges from inside to outside with a spatula to allow raw egg to cook through the edges.
5. Flip the omelet and place it over the pan. Do it upside down and then back to the pan.
6. Let sit for another 1-2 minutes.
7. Fold in half and serve.

NUTRITION:

- Calories: 90 kcal
- Fat: 2.44 g
- Carbohydrate: 15.97 g
- Protein: 8.07 g
- Sodium: 227 mg
- Potassium: 244.24 mg
- Phosphorus: 45.32 mg

17. Breakfast Maple Sausage

Preparation Time: 5 minutes
Cooking Time: 8 minutes
Servings: 12

INGREDIENTS:

- 1 lb. pork, minced
- ½-lb. lean turkey meat, ground
- ¼ tsp. nutmeg
- ½ tsp. black pepper
- ¼ allspice
- 2 tbsp. maple syrup
- 1 tbsp. water

DIRECTIONS:

1. Put the ingredients in a bowl.
2. Place a cover and put it in the fridge for 3-4 hours.
3. Take the mixture and form it into small flat patties with your hand (around 10-12 patties).
4. Lightly grease a medium skillet with oil and shallow fry the patties over medium to high heat, until brown (around 4-5 minutes on each side).
5. Serve hot.

NUTRITION:

- Calories: 53.85 kcal
- Fat: 0.9 g
- Carbohydrate: 2.42 g
- Protein: 8.5 g
- Sodium: 30.96 mg
- Potassium: 84.68 mg
- Phosphorus: 83.49 mg

18. Fast Microwave Egg Scramble

Preparation Time: 3 minutes
Cooking Time: 2 minutes
Servings: 1
INGREDIENTS:

- 1 large egg
- 2 large egg whites
- 2 tbsp. milk
- Kosher pepper, ground

DIRECTIONS:

1. Spray a coffee cup with a bit of cooking spray.
2. Whisk all the ingredients together and place them into the coffee cup.
3. Place the cup with the eggs into the microwave and set to cook for approx. 45 seconds. Take out and stir.
1. Take back in the microwave and cook for another 30 seconds.
4. Serve.

NUTRITION:

- Calories: 128.6 kcal
- Fat: 5.96 g
- Carbohydrate: 2.47 g

- Protein: 12.96 g
- Sodium: 286.36 mg
- Potassium: 185.28 mg
- Phosphorus: 122.22 mg

19. American Blueberry Pancakes

Preparation Time: 5 minutes
Cooking Time: 10 minutes
Servings: 6
INGREDIENTS:

- 1 ½ cups all-purpose flour, strain
- 1 cup buttermilk
- 3 tbsp. sugar
- 2 tbsp. butter, unsalted and melted
- 2 tsp. baking powder
- 2 eggs, beaten
- 1 cup blueberries, canned and rinsed

DIRECTIONS:

1. Prepare flour, baking powder, and sugar in a bowl.
2. Make a hole in the center and slowly add the rest of the ingredients.
3. Begin to stir gently from the sides to the center with a spatula until you get a smooth and creamy batter.
4. Put cooking spray in a small pan and place over medium heat.
5. Take one measuring cup and fill ⅓ of its capacity with the batter to make each pancake.
6. Use a spoon to pour the pancake batter and let cook until golden brown. Flip once to cook the other side.
7. Serve warm with optional agave syrup.

NUTRITION:

- Calories: 251.69 kcal
- Fat: 6.47 g
- Carbohydrate: 41.68 g
- Protein: 7.2 g
- Sodium: 186.68 mg
- Potassium: 142.87 mg
- Phosphorus: 255.39 mg

20. Mexican Scrambled Eggs in Tortilla

Preparation Time: 5 minutes
Cooking Time: 2 minutes
Servings: 2
INGREDIENTS:

- 2 medium corn tortillas
- 4 egg whites
- 1 tsp. cumin
- 3 tsp. green chilies, diced

- ½ tsp. hot pepper sauce
- 2 tbsp. salsa
- ½ tsp. salt

DIRECTIONS:
1. Spray some cooking spray on a medium skillet and heat for a few seconds.
2. Whisk the eggs with green chilies, hot sauce, and cumin.
3. Add the eggs into the pan and whisk with a spatula to scramble. Add the salt.
4. Cook until fluffy and done (1-2 minutes) over low heat.
5. Open the tortillas and spread 1 tbsp. of salsa on each.
6. Distribute the egg mixture onto the tortillas and wrap gently to make a burrito.
7. Serve warm.

NUTRITION:
- Calories: 44.1 kcal
- Fat: 0.39 g
- Carbohydrate: 2.23 g
- Protein: 7.69 g
- Sodium: 854 mg
- Potassium: 189 mg
- Phosphorus: 22 mg
- Potassium: 168.74 mg
- Phosphorus: 50.8 mg

21. Egg White and Broccoli Omelet

Preparation Time: 5 minutes
Cooking Time: 4 minutes
Servings: 2
INGREDIENTS:

- 4 egg whites
- ⅓ cup broccoli, boiled
- ½ tsp. Dill
- 1 tbsp. parmesan cheese, grated
- Salt/Pepper

DIRECTIONS:
1. Put egg whites in a bowl. Mix until stiff and white.
2. Add the dill, the broccoli, and the parmesan cheese, and incorporate everything with a spatula (do not over whisk).
3. Prepare the pan with a bit of cooking spray. Pour the egg and broccoli mixture. Cook around 1-2 minutes on each side.
4. Turn the omelet in half and optionally garnish with just a little bit of cheese on top.

NUTRITION:
- Calories: 56.82 kcal
- Fat: 1.65 g
- Carbohydrate: 2.7 g
- Protein: 10.57 g
- Sodium: 271.9 mg

APPETIZERS RECIPES

22.Cheesy Broccoli Bites

Preparation Time: 10 minutes
Cooking Time: 25 minutes
Servings: 6
INGREDIENTS:

- 2 tbsp. olive oil
- 2 heads broccoli, trimmed
- 1 egg
- ⅓ cup Cheddar cheese, reduced-fat, shredded
- 1 egg white
- ½ cup onion, chopped
- ⅓ cup breadcrumbs
- ¼ tsp. salt
- ¼ tsp. black pepper

DIRECTIONS:

1. Ready the oven at 400°F (205°C). Coat a large baking sheet with olive oil.
2. Arrange a colander in a saucepan, then place the broccoli in the colander. Pour the water into the saucepan to cover the bottom. Boil, then reduce the heat to low. Close and simmer for 6 minutes. Allow cooling for 10 minutes.
3. Blend broccoli and the remaining ingredients in a food processor. Let sit for 10 minutes.
4. Make the bites: Drop 1 tbsp. of the mixture on the baking sheet. Repeat with the remaining mixture.
1. In a preheated oven, bake for 25 minutes. Flip the bites halfway through the cooking time.
5. Serve immediately.

NUTRITION:

- Calories: 100 kcal
- Carbohydrates: 13 g
- Fiber: 3 g

23.Easy Caprese Skewers

Preparation Time: 5 minutes
Cooking Time: 0 minute
Servings: 2
INGREDIENTS:

- 12 cherry tomatoes
- 8 (1-inch) pieces Mozzarella cheese
- 12 basil leaves
- ¼ cup Italian Vinaigrette for serving

DIRECTIONS:

1. Thread the tomatoes, cheese, and bay leave alternatively through the skewers.
2. Place the skewers on a huge plate and baste with the Italian Vinaigrette. Serve immediately.

NUTRITION:

- Calories: 230 kcal
- Carbohydrates: 8.5 g
- Fiber: 1.9 g

24.Grilled Tofu with Sesame Seeds

Preparation Time: 45 minutes
Cooking Time: 20 minutes
Servings: 6
INGREDIENTS:

- 1½ tbsp. cauliflower rice vinegar
- 1 scallion
- 1 tbsp. ginger root
- 1 tbsp. applesauce, no-sugar-added
- 2 tbsp. naturally brewed soy sauce
- ¼ tsp. red pepper flakes, dried
- 2 tsp. sesame oil, toasted
- 1 (14-oz./397-g) package extra-firm tofu
- 2 tbsp. fresh cilantro
- 1 tsp. sesame seeds

DIRECTIONS:

1. Combine the vinegar, scallion, ginger, applesauce, soy sauce, red pepper flakes, and sesame oil in a large bowl. Stir to mix well.
2. Dunk the tofu pieces in the bowl, then refrigerate to marinate for 30 minutes.
3. Preheat a grill pan over medium-high heat.
4. Place the tofu on the grill pan with tongs, reserve the marinade, then grill for 8 minutes. Wait until the tofu is golden brown and has deep grilled marks on both sides.
1. Flip the tofu halfway through the cooking time.
5. Transfer the tofu to a large plate and sprinkle with cilantro leaves and sesame seeds. Serve with the marinade alongside.

NUTRITION:

- Calories: 90 kcal
- Carbohydrates: 3 g
- Fiber: 1 g

25. Kale Chips

Preparation Time: 5 minutes
Cooking Time: 15 minutes
Servings: 1
INGREDIENTS:

- ¼ tsp. garlic powder
- Pinch cayenne to taste
- 1 tbsp. extra-virgin olive oil
- ½ tsp. sea salt, or to taste
- 1 (8-oz.) bunch kale

DIRECTIONS:

1. Prepare oven at 180°C. Line two baking sheets with parchment paper.
2. Toss the garlic powder, cayenne pepper, olive oil, and salt in a large bowl, then dunk the kale in the bowl.
3. Situate kale in a single layer on one of the baking sheets.
4. Arrange the sheet in the preheated oven and bake for 7 minutes. Take the sheet from the oven and pour the kale into the single layer of the other baking sheet.
5. Move the sheet of kale back to the oven and bake for another 7 minutes.
6. Serve immediately.

NUTRITION:

- Calories: 136 kcal
- Carbohydrates: 3 g
- Fiber: 1.1 g

26. Simple Deviled Eggs

Preparation Time: 5 minutes
Cooking Time: 8 minutes
Servings: 12
INGREDIENTS:

- 6 large eggs
- ⅛ tsp. mustard powder
- 2 tbsp. light mayonnaise

DIRECTIONS:

1. Sit the eggs in a saucepan, then pour in enough water to cover the egg. Bring to a boil, then boil the eggs for another 8 minutes. Turn off the heat and cover, then let sit for 15 minutes.
2. Transfer the boiled eggs to a pot of cold water and peel them under the water.
3. Transfer the eggs to a large plate, then cut them in half. Remove the egg yolks and place them in a bowl, then mash with a fork.
4. Add the mustard powder, mayo, salt, and pepper to the bowl of yolks, then stir to mix well.
5. Spoon the yolk mixture in the egg white on the plate. Serve immediately.

NUTRITION:

- Calories: 45 kcal
- Carbohydrates: 1 g
- Fiber: 0.9 g

27. Sautéed Collard Greens and Cabbage

Preparation Time: 10 minutes
Cooking Time: 10 minutes
Servings: 8
INGREDIENTS:

- 2 tbsp. extra-virgin olive oil
- 1 collard greens bunch
- ½ small green cabbage
- 6 garlic cloves
- 1 tbsp. low-sodium soy sauce

DIRECTIONS:

1. Cook olive oil in a large skillet over medium-high heat.
2. Sauté the collard greens in the oil for about 2 minutes, or until the greens start to wilt.
3. Toss in the cabbage and mix well. Set to medium-low, cover, and cook for 5 to 7 minutes, stirring occasionally, or until the greens are softened.
4. Fold in the garlic and soy sauce and stir to combine. Cook for about 30 seconds more until fragrant.
5. Remove from the heat to a plate and serve.

NUTRITION:

- Calories: 73 kcal
- Carbohydrates: 5.9 g
- Fiber: 2.9 g

28.Roasted Delicata Squash with Thyme

Preparation Time: 10 minutes
Cooking Time: 20 minutes
Servings: 4
INGREDIENTS:

- 1 (1 ½-lb.) Delicata squash
- 1 tbsp. extra-virgin olive oil
- ½ tsp. thyme, dried
- ¼ tsp. salt
- ¼ tsp. black pepper, freshly ground

DIRECTIONS:

1. 1.Prep the oven to 400ºF (205ºC). Ready baking sheet with parchment paper and set aside.
2. Add the squash strips, olive oil, thyme, salt, and pepper in a large bowl, and toss until the squash strips are fully coated.
3. Place the squash strips on the prepared baking sheet in a single layer. Roast for about 20 minutes, flipping the strips halfway through.
4. Remove from the oven and serve on plates.

NUTRITION:

- Calories: 78 kcal
- Carbohydrates: 11.8 g
- Fiber: 2.1 g

29.Roasted Asparagus and Red Peppers

Preparation Time: 5 minutes
Cooking Time: 15 minutes
Servings: 4
INGREDIENTS:

- 1-lb. (454 g) asparagus
- 2 red bell peppers, seeded
- 1 small onion
- 2 tbsp. Italian dressing

DIRECTIONS:

1. Set the oven to 205ºC. Wrap baking sheet with parchment paper and set aside.
2. Combine the asparagus with the peppers, onion, dressing in a large bowl, and toss well.
3. Prepare the vegetables on the baking sheet and roast for about 15 minutes. Flip the vegetables with a spatula once during cooking.
4. Move to a large platter and serve.

NUTRITION:

- Calories: 92 kcal
- Carbohydrates: 10.7 g
- Fiber: 4 g

30.Tarragon Spring Peas

Preparation Time: 10 minutes
Cooking Time: 12 minutes
Servings: 6
INGREDIENTS:

- 1 tbsp. butter, unsalted
- ½ Vidalia onion
- 1 cup low-sodium vegetable broth
- 3 cups fresh peas, shelled
- 1 tbsp. fresh tarragon, minced

DIRECTIONS:

1. Cook butter in a pan at medium heat.
2. Sauté the onion in the melted butter for about 3 minutes, stirring occasionally.
3. Pour in the vegetable broth and whisk well. Add the peas and tarragon to the skillet and stir to combine.
1. Change the heat to low, cover, cook for about 8 minutes more, or until the peas are tender.
4. Let the peas cool for 5 minutes and serve warm.

NUTRITION:

- Calories: 82 kcal
- Carbohydrates: 12 g
- Fiber: 3.8 g

31.Butter-Orange Yams

Preparation Time: 7 minutes
Cooking Time: 45 minutes
Servings: 8
INGREDIENTS:

- 2 medium jewel yams
- 2 tbsp. butter, unsalted

- Juice of 1 large orange
- 1½ tsp. cinnamon, ground
- ¼ tsp. ginger, ground
- ¾ tsp. nutmeg, ground
- ⅛ tsp. cloves, ground

DIRECTIONS:

1. Set oven at 180ºC.
2. Arrange the yam dice on a rimmed baking sheet in a single layer. Set aside.
3. Add the butter, orange juice, cinnamon, ginger, nutmeg, and garlic cloves to a medium saucepan over medium-low heat.
5. Cook for 5 minutes, stirring continuously.
4. Spoon the sauce over the yams and toss to coat well.
5. Bake in the prepared oven for 40 minutes.
6. Let the yams cool for 8 minutes on the baking sheet before removing and serving.

NUTRITION:

- Calories: 129 kcal
- Carbohydrates: 24.7 g
- Fiber: 5 g

32. Roasted Tomato Brussels Sprouts

Preparation Time: 15 minutes
Cooking Time: 20 minutes
Servings: 4
INGREDIENTS:

- 1-lb. (454 g) Brussels sprouts
- 1 tbsp. extra-virgin olive oil
- ½ cup sun-dried tomatoes
- 2 tbsp. lemon juice
- 1 tsp. lemon zest

DIRECTIONS:

1. Set oven 205ºC. Prep large baking sheet with aluminum foil.
2. Put brussels sprouts in the olive oil in a large bowl until well coated. Sprinkle with salt and pepper.
3. Spread out the seasoned Brussels sprouts on the prepared baking sheet in a single layer.
4. Roast for 20 minutes, shaking halfway through.

5. Remove from the oven, then situate in a bowl—whisk tomatoes, lemon juice, and lemon zest to incorporate. Serve immediately.

NUTRITION:

- Calories: 111 kcal
- Carbohydrates: 13.7 g
- Fiber: 4.9 g

33. Green Beans in Oven

Preparation Time: 5 minutes
Cooking Time: 17 minutes
Servings: 3
INGREDIENTS:

- 12 oz. green bean pods
- 1 tbsp. olive oil
- ½ tsp. onion powder
- ⅛ tsp. pepper
- ⅛ tsp. salt

DIRECTIONS:

1. Preheat oven to 350ºF. Mix green beans with onion powder, pepper, and oil.
2. Spread the seeds on the baking sheet.
3. Bake for 17 minutes or until you have a delicious aroma in the kitchen.

NUTRITION:

- Calories: 37 kcal
- Protein: 1.4 g
- Carbohydrates: 5.5 g

34. Cream of Watercress

Preparation Time: 10 minutes
Cooking Time: 30 minutes
Servings: 2
INGREDIENTS:

- Black pepper, freshly ground
- ½ tsp. olive oil
- 6 garlic cloves
- 1 tsp. butter, unsalted
- 4 cups watercress, chopped.
- ½ sweet onion, chopped.
- ¼ cup fresh parsley, chopped.
- ¼ cup heavy cream
- 3 cups water
- 1 tbsp. lemon juice, freshly squeezed.

DIRECTIONS:

1. Preheat the oven to 400ºF.

2. On a piece of aluminum foil, put the garlic. Drizzle the foil with the olive oil and roll it into a small packet. Put that packet in a pie dish and cook the garlic for around 5 minutes or until very tender.
3. Take the garlic from the oven; cool it aside.
4. In a wide saucepan over medium to high heat, melt the butter. Sauté the onion until tender, or around 4 minutes. Add the cress and parsley and sauté for five minutes.
5. Mix in the water and the pulp of the roasted garlic. Boil the broth, then reduce the heat to a low amount.
6. Simmer the broth until the vegetables are soft or for around 20 minutes.
7. Cool the soup for approximately 5 minutes, then blend it with the heavy cream to make a puree.
8. Shift the soup to the pot and put it on low heat until it is warmed up.
9. Season with pepper and add lemon juice.

NUTRITION:

- Calories: 190 kcal
- Fat: 13 g
- Carbs: 14 g
- Protein: 4 g
- Sodium: 89 mg
- Potassium: 227 mg
- Phosphorus: 67 mg

35. Baked Garlic

Preparation Time: 10 minutes
Cooking Time: 45 minutes
Servings: 2
INGREDIENTS:

- Toasted bread (French bread or baguette)
- Small, covered baking dish
- 4 whole bulbs or heads of garlic
- 1 tsp. oregano or rosemary: dried
- 1 tbsp. olive oil

DIRECTIONS:

1. Prepare oven to 375°F.
2. To expose cloves, cut the tops off the garlic bulbs (around ½-inch)
3. Bake wrapped for 30–45 minutes, basting regularly. Spray with oil and season with herbs.
4. Squeeze the garlic from the skin and eat it. Spread or use as a basis for wonderful sauces on your favorite crusty bread.

NUTRITION:

- Calories: 33 kcal
- Fat: 3 g
- Carbs: 2 g
- Protein: 0 g
- Sodium: 1 mg
- Potassium: 26 mg
- Phosphorus: 9 mg

36. Mexican Nibbles

Preparation Time: 10 minutes
Cooking Time: 15 minutes
Servings: 2
INGREDIENTS:

- 2 ½ tsp. chili powder
- 1 egg white, room temperature
- ½ tsp. cumin
- 3 cups cereal
- ¼ tsp. garlic powder

DIRECTIONS:

1. Beat egg white until it is foamy.
2. In the dish, combine chili powder, cumin, and garlic powder, mix well and pour it in the egg white.
3. Simply add cereal, mix to cover softly.
4. Layer the mixture over a thinly greased sheet.
5. At 325°F, bake it for 15 minutes, keep stirring after every 5 minutes, and serve it cool or store it.

NUTRITION:

- Calories: 110 kcal
- Fat: 1 g
- Carbs: 25 g
- Protein: 2 g
- Sodium: 150 mg
- Potassium: 45 mg
- Phosphorus: 34 mg

37. Creamy Cucumber

Preparation Time: 10 minutes
Cooking Time: 10 minutes
Servings:
INGREDIENTS:

- 1 medium cucumber, finely minced, peeled, and seeded.
- ½-lb. cream cheese: softened.
- ½ tbsp. onion, minced
- ½ tbsp. mayonnaise
- ¼ tsp. salt
- ⅛ tsp. food coloring: green

DIRECTIONS:

1. Add the cream cheese, onion, mayonnaise, salt, and food coloring into a mixing container. Blend smoothly.
2. To the onion mixture, add the cucumber and stir them.

NUTRITION:

- Calories: 94 kcal
- Fat: 6 g
- Carbs: 9 g
- Protein: 1 g
- Sodium: 26 mg
- Potassium: 125 mg
- Phosphorus: 47 mg

38. Dill Nibbles

Preparation Time: 10 minutes
Cooking Time: 30 minutes
Servings: 2
INGREDIENTS:

- 5 tbsp. butter, unsalted
- ¾-lb. Chex cereal Rice
- ¾-lb. Chex cereal Corn
- 1 ½ tsp. garlic powder
- 1 medium Parmesan cheese
- 3 tsp. Dill weed, dried.
- ½ tbsp. Worcestershire sauce

DIRECTIONS:

1. Preheat the oven to 250°F.
2. In a large baking pan, add the rice and corn cereal.
3. Place the pot over medium-low heat and place the unsalted butter at the base of the pot. Heat until it melts.
4. Add the melted butter to the Worcestershire sauce, parmesan cheese, dill weed, and garlic powder. Stir well.
5. Add a quarter of the melted butter mixture in the baking pan over the rice and corn cereal. Mix evenly to coat.
1. Take to the oven and bake for 15 minutes.

6. Take the cereal mixture out of the oven and add the melted butter mixture to the cereal mixture. Thoroughly mix.
7. Transfer the pan back to the oven.
8. Bake for 15 more minutes.

Repeat steps 7 to 9 twice or before all the melted butter mixture is mixed.

NUTRITION:

- Calories: 116 kcal
- Fat: 4 g
- Carbs: 18 g
- Protein: 2 g
- Sodium: 217 mg
- Potassium: 45 mg
- Phosphorus: 34 mg

39. Crab-Stuffed Celery Logs

Preparation Time: 10 minutes
Cooking Time: 15 minutes
Servings: 2
INGREDIENTS:

- 1 tbsp. red onion
- ¼ cup crab meat
- 4 celery ribs (medium 8-inch)
- ¼ tsp. paprika
- 2 tsp. mayonnaise
- ½ tsp. lemon juice

DIRECTIONS:

1. Break Chop the ends of the celery rib. Drain the crab meat and flake it. Just mince the onion.
2. Combine the crab meat, cabbage, lemon juice, and mayonnaise in a shallow dish.
3. Using 1 tbsp. of the crab mix, fill each celery rib of celery into 3 parts.
4. Before eating, dust the crab-stuffed celery bits with paprika.

NUTRITION:

- Calories: 34 kcal
- Fat: 2 g
- Carbs: 2 g
- Protein: 2 g
- Sodium: 94 mg
- Potassium: 134 mg
- Phosphorus: 31 mg

40. Barbecue Meatballs

Preparation Time: 15 minutes
Cooking Time: 15 minutes
Servings: 2
INGREDIENTS:

- 3 lb. beef, ground
- ½ cup onion
- ½ cup rice milk, unenriched
- 2 large eggs
- 1 tbsp. thyme, dried
- 1 cup oatmeal, uncooked
- ½ tsp. pepper
- 1 tsp. oregano, dried
- ⅓ cup water
- 1 cup barbecue sauce

DIRECTIONS:

1. Preheat the oven to 375°F.
2. Slice the onions and beat the eggs.
3. Put all ingredients, except for the barbecue sauce and water, in a large bowl and mix them.
4. Place on a baking sheet and roll into 1-inch balls.
5. Bake for 15 minutes until the meatballs are fully cooked.
6. At low temperatures, combine water and barbecue sauce in a warming dish or Crockpot. Add and stir the meatballs. Cover until having to serve.

NUTRITION:

- Calories: 176 kcal
- Fat: 12 g
- Carbs: 6 g
- Protein: 11 g
- Sodium: 180 mg
- Potassium: 208 mg
- Phosphorus: 107 mg

41. Holiday Cheese Ball

Preparation Time: 10 minutes
Cooking Time: 30 minutes
Servings: 2
INGREDIENTS:

- ¼ cup Russian salad dressing
- 8 oz. cream cheese
- ⅓ cup walnuts, finely ground
- 1 tsp. onion powder

DIRECTIONS:

1. Melt the cream cheese.
2. Mix the salad dressing, onion powder, and cream cheese in a medium dish.
3. Put it in the fridge to cool for 30 minutes.
4. Shape the mixture of cheese into a ball.
5. Place the ground walnuts on a plate and roll to cover the cheese puck.
6. Cover and chill the cheese ball in plastic wrap before being ready to eat.

NUTRITION:

- Calories: 140 kcal
- Fat: 13 g
- Carbs: 4 g
- Protein: 2 g
- Sodium: 131 mg
- Potassium: 55 mg
- Phosphorus: 32 mg

42. Hula Meatballs

Preparation Time: 15 minutes
Cooking Time: 20 minutes
Servings: 2
INGREDIENTS:

- 4 tbsp. onion **powder**
- 4 large eggs
- 7 tbsp. cornstarch
- ½ tsp. nutmeg
- 2 cups bell peppers (red and green)
- 3 lb. beef, ground
- 2 tbsp. low-sodium soy sauce.
- ½ tsp. garlic powder
- ½ cup white sugar
- ⅔ cup water
- ⅓ cup vinegar
- ½ cup brown sugar
- 40 oz. pineapple chunks, canned
- 2 cups pineapple juice

DIRECTIONS:

1. Preheat the oven to 375°F.
2. Smash bell peppers and onion.
3. Combine 1 tbsp. of cornstarch, carrot, black pepper, nutmeg, garlic powder, ground beef, and eggs. Mix thoroughly.
1. Make 1-inch balls and put them on a baking sheet.
4. Bake for 10 minutes until the meatballs are thoroughly cooked.
5. Drain the pineapple juice into a measuring cup. To make 2 cups, add water.
6. Combine the remaining 6 tsp. of cornstarch, vinegar, reduced-sodium soy sauce, unpacked brown sugar, water, white sugar, and Pineapple juice. Heat until it thickens; continuously stir it. Remove from the heat.
7. In a covered heating dish or Crockpot placed on a low setting, put meatballs, gravy, pineapple bits, green and red peppers until ready to serve.

NUTRITION:

- Calories: 200 kcal
- Fat: 10 g
- Carbs: 16 g
- Protein: 11 g
- Sodium: 92 mg
- Potassium: 189 mg
- Phosphorus: 84 mg

43. Holiday Tuna Ball

Preparation Time: 15 minutes
Cooking Time: 30 minutes
Servings: 2
INGREDIENTS:

- 5 oz. tuna, canned
- 8 oz. cream cheese
- ¼ cup celery
- ⅓ cup cranberries, dried, sweetened
- ¼ tsp. cumin, ground
- 2 tbsp. red onion
- 1 tbsp. parsley, dried
- ¼ cup dry breadcrumbs

DIRECTIONS:

1. Place the cream cheese out for 30 minutes to melt.
2. Use a fork to drain canned tuna and flake it.
3. Combine the cream cheese, salmon, cranberries, celery, cumin, and onion in a mixing bowl. When well mixed, blend with an electric mixer.
4. The parsley and breadcrumbs are mixed and then placed on a tray. Form cream cheese mix into a puck and roll it to coat it with breadcrumbs.
5. Cover and refrigerate the ball in plastic wrap before being ready to eat.

NUTRITION:

- Calories: 77 kcal
- Fat: 5 g
- Carbs: 5 g
- Protein: 3 g
- Sodium: 92 mg
- Potassium: 51 mg
- Phosphorus: 38 mg

LUNCH RECIPES

44. Crispy Lemon Chicken

Preparation Time: 10 minutes
Cooking Time: 10 minutes
Servings: 6
INGREDIENTS:

- 1 lb. chicken breast, boneless and skinless
- ½ cup all-purpose flour
- 1 large egg
- ½ cup lemon juice
- 2 tbsp. water
- ¼ tsp. salt
- ¼ tsp. lemon pepper
- 1 tsp. mixed herb seasoning
- 2 tbsp. olive oil
- A few lemon slices, for garnishing
- 1 tbsp. parsley, chopped, for garnishing
- 2 cups plain white rice, cooked

DIRECTIONS:

1. Slice the chicken breast into thin and season with the herb, salt, and pepper.
2. In a small bowl, whisk together the egg with the water.
3. Keep the flour in a separate bowl.
4. Dip the chicken slices in the egg bath and then into the flour.
5. Heat your oil in a medium frying pan.
6. Shallow fry the chicken in the pan until golden brown.
7. Add the lemon juice and cook for another couple of minutes.
8. Take the chicken out of the pan and transfer it to a wide dish with paper to absorb excess oil.
9. Garnish with some chopped parsley and lemon wedges on top.

10. Serve with rice.

NUTRITION:

- Calories: 232 kcal
- Carbohydrate: 24 g
- Protein: 18 g
- Fat: 8 g
- Sodium: 100 g
- Potassium: 234 mg
- Phosphorus: 217 mg

45. Mexican Steak Tacos

Preparation Time: 10 minutes
Cooking Time: 15 minutes
Servings: 8
INGREDIENTS:

- 1 lb. flank or skirt steak
- ¼ cup fresh cilantro, chopped
- ¼ cup white onion, chopped
- 3 limes, juiced
- 3 garlic cloves, minced
- 2 tsp. garlic powder
- 2 tbsp. olive oil
- ½ cup Mexican or mozzarella cheese, grated
- 1 tsp. Mexican seasoning
- 8 medium-sized (6-inch) corn flour tortillas

DIRECTIONS:

1. Combine the juice from two limes, Mexican seasoning, and garlic powder in a dish or bowl and marinate the steak with it for at least half an hour in the fridge.
1. Get another bowl, combine the chopped cilantro, garlic, onion, and juice from one lime to make your salsa. Cover and keep in the fridge.
2. Slice steak into thin strips and cook for approximately 3 minutes on each side.
3. Preheat your oven to 350°F/180°C.
4. Distribute the steak strips evenly in each tortilla. Top with a tbsp. of grated cheese on top.
5. Wrap each taco in aluminum foil and bake in the oven for 7-8 minutes or until cheese is melted.
6. Serve warm with your cilantro salsa.

NUTRITION:

- Calories: 230 kcal
- Carbohydrate: 19.5 g
- Protein: 15 g
- Fat: 11 g
- Sodium: 486.75 g
- Potassium: 240 mg
- Phosphorus: 268 mg

46. Beer Pork Ribs

Preparation Time: 10 minutes
Cooking Time: 8 hours
Servings: 1
INGREDIENTS:

- 2 lb. pork ribs, cut into two units/racks
- 18 oz. root beer
- 2 garlic cloves, minced
- 2 tbsp. onion powder
- 2 tbsp. vegetable oil (optional)

DIRECTIONS:

1. Wrap the pork ribs with vegetable oil and place one unit on the bottom of your slow cooker with half of the minced garlic and the onion powder.
2. Place the other rack on top with the rest of the garlic and onion powder.
3. Pour over the root beer and cover the lid.
4. Let simmer for 8 hours on low heat.
5. Take off and finish optionally in a grilling pan for a nice sear.

NUTRITION:

- Calories: 301 kcal
- Carbohydrate: 36 g
- Protein: 21 g
- Fat: 18 g
- Sodium: 729 mg
- Potassium: 200 mg
- Phosphorus: 209 mg

47. Mexican Chorizo Sausage

Preparation Time: 10 minutes
Cooking Time: 15 minutes
Servings: 1
INGREDIENTS:

- 2 lb. pork, boneless, but coarsely ground
- 3 tbsp. red wine vinegar

- 2 tbsp. paprika, smoked
- ½ tsp. cinnamon
- ½ tsp. cloves, ground
- ¼ tsp. coriander seeds
- ¼ tsp. ginger, ground
- 1 tsp. cumin, ground
- 3 tbsp. brandy

DIRECTIONS:

1. Prepare a large mixing bowl, combine the ground pork with the seasonings, brandy, and vinegar and mix with your hands well.
2. Place the mixture into a large Ziploc bag and leave it in the fridge overnight.
3. Form into 15-16 patties of equal size.
4. In a large pan, warm the oil and fry the patties for 5-7 minutes on each side, or until the meat inside is no longer pink and there is a light brown crust on top.
5. Serve hot.

NUTRITION:

- Calories: 134 kcal
- Carbohydrate: 0 g
- Protein: 10 g
- Fat: 7 g
- Sodium: 40 mg
- Potassium: 138 mg
- Phosphorus: 128 mg

48. Italian Meatballs

Preparation Time: 15 minutes
Cooking Time: 15 minutes
Servings: 2
INGREDIENTS:

- 3 large eggs
- 1 cup onion
- 1 tbsp. garlic powder
- 3 lb. beef, ground
- 1 tbsp. olive oil
- 1 cup oatmeal, uncooked
- 6 tbsp. parmesan cheese
- 1 tsp. black pepper, ground
- 2 tsp. oregano, dried
- 1 cup Roasted Red Pepper Tomato Sauce

DIRECTIONS:

1. Make a Roasted Red Pepper Tomato Sauce and put it aside.
2. Prepare the oven to 375°F and cut onions.
3. In a large bowl, beat the eggs, then add all the ingredients and blend.

4. Put on a baking sheet and roll into 1-inch balls.
5. Bake for 15 minutes, till the meatballs are thoroughly cooked.
6. To serve, put meatballs on a low heat setting in a cooking pan or slow cooker. Serve with sauce and noodles.

NUTRITION:

- Calories: 160 kcal
- Fat: 11 g
- Carbs: 3 g
- Protein: 12 g
- Sodium: 54 mg
- Potassium: 133 mg
- Phosphorus: 99 mg

49. Eggplant Casserole

Preparation Time: 10 minutes
Cooking Time: 25–30 minutes
Servings: 4
INGREDIENTS:

- 3 cups eggplant, peeled and cut into large chunks
- 2 egg whites
- 1 large egg, whole
- ½ cup vegetable, unsweetened
- ¼ tsp. sage
- ½ cup breadcrumbs
- 1 tbsp. margarine, melted
- ¼ tsp. garlic salt

DIRECTIONS:

1. Preheat the oven at 350°F/180°C.
2. Place the eggplants chunks in a medium pan, cover with a bit of water and cook with the lid covered until tender. Drain from the water and mash with a tool or fork.
3. Beat the eggs with non-dairy vegetable cream, sage, salt, and pepper. Whisk in the eggplant mush.
4. Put together the melted margarine with the breadcrumbs.
5. Bake in the oven for 20-25 minutes or until the casserole has a golden-brown crust.

NUTRITION:

- Calories: 186 kcal
- Carbohydrate: 19 g
- Protein: 7 g
- Fat: 9 g
- Sodium: 503 mg
- Potassium: 230 mg
- Phosphorus: 62 mg

50. Mexican Style Burritos

Preparation Time: 5 minutes
Cooking Time: 15 minutes
Servings: 2
INGREDIENTS:

- 1 tbsp. olive oil
- 2 corn tortillas
- ¼ cup red onion, chopped
- ¼ cup red bell peppers, chopped
- ½, red chili, deseeded and chopped
- 2 eggs
- 1 lime juice
- 1 tbsp. cilantro, chopped

DIRECTIONS:

1. Place the tortillas on medium heat for 1 to 2 minutes on each side or until lightly toasted.
2. Remove and keep the broiler on.
3. On a heated skillet, put oil and sauté onion, chili, and bell peppers for 5 minutes or until soft.
4. Crack the eggs over the top of the onions and peppers.
5. Place skillet under the broiler for 5 to 6 minutes or until the eggs are cooked.
6. Serve half the eggs and vegetables on top of each tortilla and sprinkle with cilantro and lime juice to serve.

NUTRITION:

- Calories: 202 kcal
- Fat: 13 g
- Carb: 19 g
- Protein: 9 g
- Sodium: 77 mg
- Potassium: 233 mg
- Phosphorus: 184 mg

51. Pizza with Chicken and Pesto

Preparation Time: 10 minutes
Cooking Time: 25 minutes
Servings: 4
INGREDIENTS:

- 1 ready-made pizza dough, frozen

- ⅔ cup chicken, cooked and chopped
- ½ cup green bell pepper, diced
- ½ cup orange bell pepper, diced
- ¼ cup purple onion, chopped
- 2 tbsp. green basil pesto
- 1 tbsp. chives, chopped
- ⅓ cup parmesan or Romano cheese, grated
- ¼ cup mozzarella cheese
- 1 tbsp. olive oil

DIRECTIONS:

1. Thaw the pizza dough according to directions on the package.
2. Heat the olive oil in a pan and sauté the peppers and onions for a couple of minutes. Set aside
3. Once the pizza dough has thawed, spread the Bali pesto over its surface.
4. Top with half of the cheese, the peppers, the onions, and the chicken. Finish with the rest of the cheese.
5. Bake at 350°F/180°C for approximately 20 minutes (or until crust and cheese are baked).
6. Slice in triangles with a pizza cutter or sharp knife and serve.

NUTRITION:

- Calories: 225 kcal
- Carbohydrate: 13.9 g
- Protein: 11.1 g
- Fat: 12 g
- Sodium: 321 mg
- Potassium: 174 mg
- Phosphorus: 172 mg

52. Shrimp Quesadilla

Preparation Time: 10 minutes
Cooking Time: 10 minutes
Servings: 2
INGREDIENTS:

- 5 oz. shrimp, shelled and deveined
- 4 tbsp. Mexican salsa
- 2 tbsp. fresh cilantro, chopped
- 1 tbsp. lemon juice
- 1 tsp. cumin, ground
- 1 tsp. cayenne pepper
- 2 tbsp. soy yogurt or creamy tofu, unsweetened
- 2 medium corn flour tortillas
- 2 tbsp. cheddar cheese, low-fat

DIRECTIONS:

1. Mix the cilantro, cumin, lemon juice, and cayenne in a Ziploc bag to make your marinade.

2. Put the shrimps and marinate for 10 minutes.
6. In the pan, put the oil on medium heat and toss the shrimp with the marinade. Cook for more minutes or as soon as shrimps have turned pink and opaque.
3. Add the soy cream or soft tofu to the pan and mix well. Remove from the heat and keep the marinade aside.
4. Heat tortillas in the grill or microwave for a few seconds.
5. Place 2 tbsp. of salsa on each tortilla. Top one tortilla with the shrimp mixture and add the cheese on top.
6. Stack one tortilla against each other (with the spread salsa layer facing the shrimp mixture).
7. Transfer this to a baking tray and cook for 7-8 minutes at 350°F/180°C to melt the cheese and crisp up the tortillas.
8. Serve warm.

NUTRITION:

- Calories: 255 kcal
- Carbohydrate: 21 g
- Fat: 9 g
- Protein: 24 g
- Sodium: 562 g
- Potassium: 235 mg
- Phosphorus: 189 mg

53. Grilled Corn on the Cob

Preparation Time: 5 minutes
Cooking Time: 20 minutes
Servings: 4
INGREDIENTS:

- 4 corn on the cob, frozen, cut in half
- ½ tsp. thyme
- 1 tbsp. parmesan cheese, grated
- ¼ tsp. black pepper

DIRECTIONS:

1. Combine the oil, cheese, thyme, and black pepper in a bowl.
2. Place the corn in the cheese/oil mix and roll to coat evenly.
3. Fold all 4 pieces in aluminum foil, leaving a small open surface on top.
4. Place the wrapped corns over the grill and let cook for 20 minutes.
5. Serve hot.

NUTRITION:

- Calories: 125 kcal
- Carbohydrate: 29.5 g
- Protein: 2 g
- Fat: 1.3 g
- Sodium: 26 g
- Potassium: 145 mg
- Phosphorus: 91.5 mg

54. Couscous with Veggies

Preparation Time: 10 minutes
Cooking Time: 10 minutes
Servings: 5
INGREDIENTS:

- ½ cup couscous, uncooked
- ¼ cup white mushrooms, sliced
- ½ cup red onion, chopped
- 1 garlic clove, minced
- ½ cup peas, frozen
- 2 tbsp. dry white wine
- ½ tsp. basil
- 2 tbsp. fresh parsley, chopped
- 1 cup water or vegetable stock
- 1 tbsp. margarine or vegetable oil

DIRECTIONS:

1. Thaw the peas by setting them aside at room temperature for 15-20 minutes.
2. In a medium pan, heat the margarine or vegetable oil.
3. Add the onions, peas, mushroom, and garlic and sauté for around 5 minutes. Add the wine and let it evaporate.
4. Add all the herbs and spices and toss well. Take off the heat and keep it aside.
5. In a small pot, cook the couscous with 1 cup of hot water or vegetable stock. Bring to a boil, take the heat, and sit for a few minutes with a lid covered.
6. Add the sauté veggies to the couscous and toss well.
7. Serve in a serving bowl, warm or cold.

NUTRITION:

- Calories: 110.4 kcal
- Carbohydrate: 18 g
- Protein: 3 g
- Fat: 2 g
- Sodium: 112.2 mg
- Potassium: 69.6 mg
- Phosphorus: 46.8 mg

55. Easy Egg Salad

Preparation Time: 5 minutes
Cooking Time: 8 minutes
Servings: 4
INGREDIENTS:

- 4 large eggs
- ½ cup sweet onion, chopped
- ¼ cup celery, chopped
- 2 tbsp. pickle relish
- 1 tbsp. yellow mustard
- 1 tsp. paprika, smoked
- 3 tbsp. mayo

DIRECTIONS:

1. Hard boil the eggs in a small pot filled with water for approx. 7-8 minutes. Leave the eggs in the water for an extra couple of minutes before peeling.
2. Peel the eggs and chop finely with a knife or tool.
3. Combine all the chopped veggies with mayo and mustard. Add in the eggs and mix well.
4. Sprinkle with some smoked paprika on top.
5. Serve cold with pitta, white bread slices, or lettuce wraps.

NUTRITION:

- Calories: 127 kcal
- Carbohydrate: 6 g
- Protein: 7 g
- Fat: 13 g
- Sodium: 170.7 mg
- Potassium: 87.5 mg
- Phosphorus: 101 mg

56. Cucumber Sandwich

Preparation Time: 1 hour
Cooking Time: 5 minutes
Servings: 2
INGREDIENTS:

- 6 tsp. cream cheese
- 1 pinch dill weed, dried
- 3 tsp. mayonnaise
- ¼ tsp. dry Italian dressing mix
- 4 slices white bread
- ½ of a cucumber

DIRECTIONS:

1. Prepare the cucumber and cut it into slices.
2. Mix cream cheese, mayonnaise, and Italian dressing. Chill for 1 hour.
3. Distribute the mixture onto the white bread slices.
4. Place cucumber slices on top and sprinkle with the dill weed.
5. Cut in halves and serve.

NUTRITION:

- Calories: 143 kcal
- Fat: 6 g
- Carbs: 16.7 g
- Protein: 4 g
- Sodium: 255 mg
- Potassium: 127 mg
- Phosphorus: 64 mg

57. Pizza Pitas

Preparation Time: 10 minutes
Cooking Time: 10 minutes
Servings: 1
INGREDIENTS:

- .33 cup mozzarella cheese
- 2 pieces pita bread, 6 inches in size
- 6 tsp. chunky tomato sauce
- 2 garlic cloves, minced
- ¼ cups onion, chopped small
- ¼ tsp. red pepper flakes
- ¼ cup bell pepper, chopped small
- 2 oz. pork lean, ground
- No-stick oil spray
- ½ tsp. fennel seeds

DIRECTIONS:

1. Preheat oven to 400°F.
2. Put the garlic, ground meat, pepper flakes, onion, and bell pepper in a pan. Sauté until cooked.
3. Grease a flat baking pan and put pitas on it. Use the mixture to spread on the pita bread.
4. Spread 1 tbsp. of the tomato sauce and top with cheese.
5. Bake for 5 to 8 minutes until the cheese is bubbling.

NUTRITION:

- Calories: 284 kcal
- Fat: 10 g
- Carbs: 34 g
- Protein: 16 g
- Sodium: 795 mg
- Potassium: 706 mg
- Phosphorus: 416 mg

58. Turkey Pinwheels

Preparation Time: 10 minutes
Cooking Time: 15 minutes
Servings: 6
INGREDIENTS:

- 6 toothpicks
- 8 oz. spring mix salad greens
- 1 (10-inch) tortilla
- 2 oz. deli turkey, thinly sliced
- 9 tsp. cream cheese, whipped
- 1 red bell pepper, roasted

DIRECTIONS:

1. Cut the red bell pepper into ten strips about a quarter-inch thick.
2. Spread the whipped cream cheese on the tortilla evenly.
3. Add the salad greens to create a base layer, and then lay the turkey on top.
4. Space out the red bell pepper strips on top of the turkey.
5. Tuck the end and begin rolling the tortilla inward.
6. Use the toothpicks to hold the roll into place and cut it into six pieces.
7. Serve with the swirl facing upward.

NUTRITION:

- Calories: 206 kcal
- Fat: 9 g
- Carbs: 21 g
- Protein: 9 g
- Sodium: 533 mg
- Potassium: 145 mg
- Phosphorus: 47 mg

59. Chicken Tacos

Preparation Time: 5 minutes
Cooking Time: 20 minutes
Servings: 4
INGREDIENTS:

- · 8 corn tortillas
- 1 ½ tsp. taco seasoning, sodium-free
- 1 juiced lime
- ½ cups cilantro
- 2 pieces green onions, chopped
- 8 oz. romaine lettuce, shredded or chopped
- ¼ cup sour cream
- 1 lb. chicken breast, boneless and skinless

DIRECTIONS:

1. Cook chicken, by boiling, for twenty minutes. Shred or chop cooked chicken into fine bite-sized pieces.
2. Mix the seasoning and lime juice with the chicken.
3. Put chicken mixture and lettuce in tortillas.
4. Top with green onions, cilantro, sour cream.

NUTRITION:

- Calories: 260 kcal
- Fat: 3 g
- Carbs: 36 g
- Protein: 23 g
- Sodium: 922 mg
- Potassium: 445 mg
- Phosphorus: 357 mg

60. Ciabatta Rolls with Chicken Pesto

Preparation Time: 10 minutes
Cooking Time: 20 minutes
Servings: 2
INGREDIENTS:

- 6 tsp. Greek yogurt
- 6 tsp. pesto
- 2 small ciabatta rolls
- 8 oz. iceberg or romaine lettuce, shredded
- 8 oz. chicken breast, cooked, boneless, and skinless, shredded
- .125 tsp. pepper

DIRECTIONS:

1. Combine the shredded chicken, pesto, pepper, and Greek yogurt in a medium-sized bowl.
2. Slice and toast the ciabatta rolls.
3. Divide the shredded chicken and pesto mixture in half and make sandwiches with the ciabatta rolls.
4. Top with shredded lettuce if desired.

NUTRITION:

- Calories: 374 kcal
- Fat: 10 g
- Carbs: 40 g
- Protein: 30 g
- Sodium: 522 mg
- Potassium: 360 mg
- Phosphorus: 84 mg

61. Marinated Shrimp Pasta Salad

Preparation Time: 15 minutes
Cooking Time: 5 hours
Servings: 1
INGREDIENTS:

- ¼ cup honey
- ¼ cup balsamic vinegar
- ½ an English cucumber, cubed
- ½ lb. fully cooked shrimp
- 15 baby carrots
- 1½ cups cauliflower, dime-sized cut
- 4 stalks celery, diced
- ½ large yellow bell pepper, diced
- ½ red onion, diced
- ½ large red bell pepper, diced
- 12 oz. uncooked tri-color pasta, cooked
- ¾ cup olive oil
- 3 tsp. Dijon mustard
- ½ tsp. garlic powder
- ½ tsp. pepper

DIRECTIONS:

1. Cut vegetables and put them in a bowl with the shrimp.
2. Whisk the honey, balsamic vinegar, garlic powder, pepper, and Dijon mustard in a small bowl. Slowly add the oil while still whisking and mix it all.
3. Add the cooked pasta to the bowl with the shrimp and vegetables and mix it.
4. Toss the sauce to coat the pasta, shrimp, and vegetables evenly.
5. Cover and chill for a minimum of five hours before serving. Stir and serve while chilled.

NUTRITION:

- Calories: 205 kcal
- Fat: 13 g
- Carbs: 10 g
- Protein: 12 g
- Sodium: 363 mg
- Potassium: 156 mg
- Phosphorus: 109 mg

62. Peanut Butter and Jelly Grilled Sandwich

Preparation Time: 5 minutes
Cooking Time: 5 minutes
Servings: 1
INGREDIENTS:

- 2 tsp. butter, unsalted
- 6 tsp. peanut butter
- 3 tsp. flavored jelly
- 2 pieces bread

DIRECTIONS:

1. Put the peanut butter evenly on one bread. Add the layer of jelly.
2. Butter the outside of the pieces of bread.
3. Add the sandwich to a frying pan and toast both sides.

NUTRITION:

- Calories: 300 kcal
- Fat: 7 g
- Carbs: 49 g
- Protein: 8 g
- Sodium: 460 mg
- Potassium: 222 mg
- Phosphorus: 80 mg

63. Grilled Onion and Pepper Jack Grilled Cheese Sandwich

Preparation Time: 5 minutes
Cooking Time: 5 minutes
Servings: 2
INGREDIENTS:

- 1 tsp. olive oil
- 6 tsp. cream cheese, whipped
- ½ of a medium onion
- 2 oz. pepper jack cheese
- 4 slices rye bread
- 2 tsp. butter, unsalted

DIRECTIONS:

1. Prepare butter so that it becomes soft. Slice up the onion into thin slices.
2. Sauté onion slices. Continue to stir until cooked. Remove and put it to the side.
3. Spread 1 tbsp. of the whipped cream cheese on two of the slices of bread.
4. Then add grilled onions and cheese to each slice. Then top using the other two bread slices.
5. Spread the softened butter on the outside of the slices of bread.
6. Use the skillet to toast the sandwiches until lightly brown, and the cheese is melted.

NUTRITION:

- Calories: 350 kcal
- Fat: 18 g
- Carbs: 34 g
- Protein: 13 g
- Sodium: 589 mg
- Potassium: 184 mg
- Phosphorus: 226 mg

64. Lettuce Wraps with Chicken

Preparation Time: 5 minutes
Cooking Time: 5 minutes
Servings: 2
INGREDIENTS:

- 8 lettuce leaves
- ¼ cups fresh cilantro
- ¼ cups mushroom
- 1 tsp. five spices seasoning
- ¼ cups onion
- 6 tsp. rice vinegar
- 2 tsp. hoisin
- 6 tsp. canola oil
- 3 tsp. sesame oil
- 2 tsp. garlic
- 2 pieces scallions
- 8 oz. chicken breast, cooked

DIRECTIONS:

1. Put the cooked chicken and the garlic together. Slice onions, cilantro, mushrooms, and scallions.
2. Use a skillet overheat, combine chicken with all remaining ingredients, minus the lettuce leaves. Cook for fifteen minutes, stirring occasionally.
3. Place ¼ cup of the mixture into each leaf of lettuce. Wrap the lettuce like a burrito and eat.

NUTRITION:

- Calories: 219 kcal
- Fat: 15 g
- Carbs: 4 g
- Protein: 17 g
- Sodium: 103 mg
- Potassium: 225 mg
- Phosphorus: 130 mg

DINNER RECIPES

65. Seafood Casserole

Preparation Time: 20 minutes
Cooking Time: 45 minutes
Servings: 1
INGREDIENTS:

- 2 cups eggplant, diced into 1-inch, peeled
- Butter, for greasing the baking dish
- 1 tbsp. Olive oil
- ½ Sweet onion, chopped
- 1 tsp. garlic, minced
- 1 celery stalk, chopped
- ½ red bell pepper, boiled and chopped
- 3 tbsp. lemon juice, freshly squeezed
- 1 tsp. hot sauce
- ¼ tsp. creole seasoning mix
- ½ cup white rice, uncooked
- 1 large egg
- 4 oz. shrimp, cooked
- 6 oz. Queen crab meat

DIRECTIONS:

1. Preheat the oven to 350°F.
2. In the saucepan, boil the eggplant for 5 minutes. Drain and set it aside.
3. Put the butter in a baking dish and set it aside.
4. Warm the olive oil in a skillet over medium heat.
5. Fry the garlic, onion, celery, and bell pepper for 4 minutes or until tender.
6. Put the cooked vegetables to the eggplant, along with the lemon juice, hot sauce, seasoning, rice, and egg.
7. Stir to combine.
8. Fold in the shrimp and crab meat.
9. Put the mixture into the casserole dish, patting down the top.

10. Bake for 30 minutes or until casserole is heated through and rice is tender. Serve warm.

NUTRITION:

- Calories: 118 kcal
- Fat: 4 g
- Carb: 9 g
- Protein: 12 g
- Sodium: 235 mg
- Potassium: 199 mg
- Phosphorus: 102 mg

66. Eggplant and Red Pepper Soup

Preparation Time: 20 minutes
Cooking Time: 40 minutes
Servings: 1
INGREDIENTS:

- 1 small sweet onion, cut into quarters
- 2 small red bell peppers, halved
- 2 cups eggplant, cubed
- 2 garlic cloves, crushed
- 1 tbsp. olive oil
- 1 cup chicken stock
- Water
- ¼ cup fresh basil, chopped
- Black pepper, ground

DIRECTIONS:

1. Preheat the oven to 350°F.
2. Add onions, red peppers, eggplant, and garlic to a baking dish.
3. Drizzle the vegetables with olive oil.
4. Cook vegetables until they are slightly charred and soft or for 30 minutes.
5. Let it cool and remove the skin from the peppers.
6. Blend vegetables with a hand mixer (with the chicken stock).
7. Put the soup in a medium pot and add enough water to reach the desired thickness.
8. Let the soup simmer and add the basil.
9. Season with pepper and serve.

NUTRITION:

- Calories: 61 kcal
- Fat: 2 g
- Carb: 9 g
- Protein: 2 g
- Sodium: 98 mg
- Potassium: 198 mg
- Phosphorus: 33 mg

67. Ground Beef and Rice Soup

Preparation Time: 15 minutes
Cooking Time: 40 minutes
Servings: 1
INGREDIENTS:

- ½-lb. extra-lean ground beef
- ½ small sweet onion, chopped
- 1 tsp. garlic, minced
- 2 cups water
- 1 cup low-sodium beef broth
- ½ cup long-grain white rice, uncooked
- 1 celery stalk, chopped
- ½ cup fresh green beans, cut into 1-inch pieces
- 1 tsp. fresh thyme, chopped
- Black pepper, ground

DIRECTIONS:

1. Sauté the ground beef in a saucepan for 6 minutes or until the beef is completely browned.
2. Remove excess fat and add the onion and garlic to the saucepan.
3. Sauté the vegetables for about 3 minutes, or until they are softened.
4. Add celery, rice, beef broth, and water.
5. Let it boil, reduce the heat to low, and simmer for 30 minutes or until the rice is tender.
6. Add the green beans and thyme and simmer for 3 minutes.
7. Remove the soup from the heat and season with pepper.

NUTRITION:

- Calories: 154 kcal
- Fat: 7 g
- Carb: 14 g
- Protein: 9 g
- Sodium: 133 mg
- Potassium: 179 mg
- Phosphorus: 76 mg

68. Couscous Burgers

Preparation Time: 20 minutes
Cooking Time: 10 minutes
Servings: 4
INGREDIENTS:

- ½ cup, canned chickpeas
- 2 tbsp. fresh cilantro, chopped
- Fresh parsley, chopped
- 1 tbsp. lemon juice
- 2 tsp. lemon zest
- 1 tsp. garlic, minced
- 2 ½ cups couscous, cooked
- 2 eggs, lightly beaten
- 2 tbsp. olive oil

DIRECTIONS:

1. Rinse and drain the canned chickpeas
2. Put the cilantro, chickpeas, parsley, lemon juice, lemon zest, and garlic in a food processor and pulse until a paste forms.
3. Put chickpea mixture in a bowl. Add the eggs and couscous. Mix well.
4. Refrigerate the mixture for 1 hour.
5. Form the couscous mixture into 4 patties.
6. Heat olive oil in a skillet.
7. Place and cook two patties in the skillet, gently pressing them down with a spatula for 5 minutes or until golden, and flip the patties over.
8. Repeat with the remaining burgers.

NUTRITION:

- Calories: 242 kcal
- Fat: 10 g
- Carb: 29 g
- Protein: 9 g
- Sodium: 43 mg
- Potassium: 168 mg
- Phosphorus: 108 mg

69. Pork Souvlaki

Preparation Time: 20 minutes
Cooking Time: 12 minutes
Servings: 8
INGREDIENTS:

- 3 tbsp. olive oil
- 2 tbsp. lemon juice
- 1 tsp. garlic, minced
- 1 tbsp. fresh oregano, chopped
- ¼ tsp. black pepper, ground
- 1 lb. pork leg, cut into 2-inch cubes

DIRECTIONS:

1. Put together the lemon juice, olive oil, garlic, oregano, and pepper in a bowl.
2. Add pork cubes and toss to coat.
3. Place the bowl in the refrigerator, covered, for 2 hours to marinate.
4. Thread the pork chunks onto 8 wooden skewers that have been soaked in water.
5. Preheat the barbecue to medium-high heat.
6. Grill the pork skewers for about 12 minutes, turning once, until just cooked through but still juicy.

NUTRITION:

- Calories: 95 kcal
- Fat: 4 g
- Carb: 0 g
- Protein: 13 g
- Sodium: 29 mg
- Potassium: 230 mg
- Phosphorus: 125 mg

70. Baked Flounder

Preparation Time: 20 minutes
Cooking Time: 5 minutes
Servings: 4
INGREDIENTS:

- ¼ cup Homemade mayonnaise
- Juice of 1 lime
- Zest of 1 lime
- ½ cup fresh cilantro, chopped
- 4 (3-oz.) flounder fillets
- Black pepper, ground

DIRECTIONS:

1. Preheat the oven to 400°F.
2. In a bowl, stir together the cilantro, lime juice, lime zest, and mayonnaise.
3. Prepare foil on a clean work surface.
4. Place a flounder fillet in the center of each square.
5. Top the fillets evenly with the mayonnaise mixture.
6. Season the flounder with pepper.
7. Fold the foil's sides over the fish and place them on a baking sheet.
8. Bake for 4–5 minutes.
9. Unfold the packets and serve.

NUTRITION:

- Calories: 92 kcal
- Fat: 4 g
- Carb: 2 g
- Protein: 12 g
- Sodium: 267 mg
- Potassium: 137 mg
- Phosphorus: 208 mg

71. Persian Chicken

Preparation Time: 10 minutes
Cooking Time: 20 minutes
Servings: 5
INGREDIENTS:

- ½, sweet onion, chopped
- ¼ cup lemon juice
- 1 tbsp. oregano, dried
- 1 tsp. garlic, minced
- 1 tsp. sweet paprika
- ½ tsp. cumin, ground
- ½ cup olive oil
- 5 chicken thighs, boneless, skinless

DIRECTIONS:

1. Put the cumin, paprika, garlic, oregano, lemon juice, and onion in a food processor and pulse to mix the ingredients.
2. Put olive oil until the mixture is smooth.
3. Put chicken thighs in a large Ziploc and add the marinade for 2 hours.
4. Remove the thighs from the marinade.
5. Preheat the barbecue to medium.
6. Grill the chicken for 20 minutes, turning once, until it reaches 165°F.

NUTRITION:

- Calories: 321 kcal
- Fat: 21 g
- Carb: 3 g
- Protein: 22 g
- Sodium: 86 mg
- Potassium: 220 mg
- Phosphorus: 131mg

72. Beef Chili

Preparation Time: 10 minutes
Cooking Time: 30 minutes
Servings: 2
INGREDIENTS:

- 1 onion, diced
- 1 red bell pepper, diced
- 2 garlic cloves, minced
- 6 oz. lean ground beef
- 1 tsp. chili powder
- 1 tsp. oregano
- 2 tbsp. extra virgin olive oil
- 1 cup water
- 1 cup cauliflower rice
- 1 tbsp. fresh cilantro to serve

DIRECTIONS:

1. Soak vegetables in warm water.
2. Boil a pan of water and put rice for 20 minutes.
3. Meanwhile, add the oil to a pan and heat it on medium heat.
4. Put pepper, onions, and garlic and sauté for 5 minutes until soft.
5. Remove and set aside.
6. In the pan, add beef and stir until browned.
7. Put and stir vegetables back into the pan.
8. Now add the chili powder and herbs and the water, cover, and turn the heat down a little to simmer for 15 minutes.
9. Meanwhile, drain the water from the rice and the lid and steam while the chili is cooking.
10. Serve hot with the fresh cilantro sprinkled over the top.

NUTRITION:

- Calories: 459 kcal
- Fat: 22 g
- Carb: 36 g
- Protein: 22 g
- Sodium: 33 mg
- Potassium: 360 mg
- Phosphorus: 332 mg

73. Pork Meatloaf

Preparation Time: 10 minutes
Cooking Time: 50 minutes
Servings: 1
INGREDIENTS:

- 1-lb. lean beef, ground
- ½ cup breadcrumbs
- ½ cup sweet onion, chopped
- 1 egg
- 2 tbsp. fresh basil, chopped
- 1 tsp. fresh thyme, chopped
- 1 tsp. fresh parsley, chopped
- ¼ tsp. black pepper, ground
- 1 tbsp. brown sugar
- 1 tsp. white vinegar
- ¼ tsp. garlic powder

DIRECTIONS:

1. Preheat the oven to 350°F.
2. Mix the breadcrumbs, beef, onion, basil, egg, thyme, parsley, and pepper well.
3. Stir the brown sugar, vinegar, and garlic powder in a small bowl.
4. Put the brown sugar mixture evenly over the meat.
5. Bake the meatloaf for about 50 minutes or until it is cooked through.
6. Leave the meatloaf for 10 minutes, and then pour out any accumulated grease.

NUTRITION:

- Calories: 103 kcal
- Fat: 3 g
- Carb: 7 g
- Protein: 11 g
- Sodium: 87 mg
- Potassium: 190 mg
- Phosphorus: 112 mg

74. Chicken Stew

Preparation Time: 20 minutes
Cooking Time: 50 minutes
Servings: 1
INGREDIENTS:

- 1 tbsp. olive oil
- 1 lb. chicken thighs, boneless, skinless, cut into 1-inch cubes
- ½ sweet onion, chopped
- 1 tbsp. garlic, minced
- 2 cups chicken stock
- 1 cup plus 2 tbsp. water
- 1 carrot, sliced
- 2 celery stalks, sliced
- 1 turnip, sliced thin
- 1 tbsp. fresh thyme, chopped
- 1 tsp. fresh rosemary, chopped
- 2 tsp. cornstarch
- Black pepper, ground, to taste

DIRECTIONS:

1. Prepare a large saucepan on medium heat and add olive oil.
2. Sauté the chicken for 6 minutes or until it is lightly browned, stirring often.
3. Add onion and garlic, then sauté for 3 minutes.
4. Add 1-cup water, chicken stock, carrot, celery, and turnip and bring the stew to a boil.
5. Simmer for 30 minutes or until cooked and tender.
6. Add the thyme and rosemary and simmer for 3 minutes more.
7. Get a small bowl, stir together the 2 tbsp. Of water and the cornstarch
8. Add the mixture to the stew.
9. Stir to incorporate the cornstarch mixture and cook for 3 to 4 minutes or until the stew thickens.
10. Remove from the heat once done and season with pepper.

NUTRITION:

- Calories: 141 kcal
- Fat: 8 g
- Carb: 5 g
- Protein: 9 g
- Sodium: 214 mg
- Potassium: 192 mg
- Phosphorus: 53 mg

75. Green Tuna Salad

Preparation Time: 10 minutes
Cooking Time: 15–20 minutes
Servings: 2
INGREDIENTS:

- 5 oz. tuna (in freshwater only)
- 2-3 cups lettuce
- ½ cup Italian tomatoes
- 1 cup baby marrows
- ½ cup red bell pepper
- ¼ cup red onion
- ¼ cup fresh thyme
- 2 tbsp. olive oil
- ⅛ tsp. black pepper
- 2 tbsp. red wine vinegar

DIRECTIONS:

1. Chop the bell pepper, onion, baby marrow, and thyme into small pieces.
2. Add ¾ cup of water to a saucepan and add the bell pepper, onion, baby marrow, and thyme to the pan. Let it boil, steam the vegetables by adding a lid on the saucepan—steam for 10 minutes.
3. Remove the vegetables and drain them.
4. Combine the vegetables (once cooled down) with chopped tomatoes and tuna.
5. Mix olive oil, red wine vinegar, and black pepper to create a salad dressing.
6. Add the mixture to a bed of lettuce and drizzle the dressing on top.

NUTRITION:

- Calories: 210 kcal
- Fat: 1.5 g
- Carbs: 4 g
- Protein: 43.3 g
- Sodium: 726 mg
- Potassium: 582 mg
- Phosphorus: 296 mg

76. Roasted Chicken and Vegetables

Preparation Time: 10 minutes
Cooking Time: 45 minutes
Servings: 2
INGREDIENTS:

- 8 oz. chicken strips
- 1 ½ cups baby potatoes
- 5 oz. green beans
- 2 tbsp. sesame seed oil
- 1 tsp. Cajun chicken spice
- ½ tbsp. Italian herb dressing

DIRECTIONS:

1. Heat the oven to 400°F.
1. Add ¾ full water to a large pot. Prepare the baby potatoes to the pot and cook for 10 minutes.
2. Drain the baby potatoes.
3. Chop off the tips of the green beans.
4. Line the oven tray with parchment paper or spray the oven tray with cooking spray.
5. Place the chicken strips on the tray side with the green beans and baby potatoes.
6. Add Cajun chicken spice to the chicken breasts and drizzle sesame seed oil over the chicken and vegetables.
7. Roast for 20 minutes.
8. Drizzle Italian herb dressing on the chicken and vegetables and roast for another 5-10 minutes.

NUTRITION:

- Calories: 263 kcal
- Fat: 6 g
- Sodium: 366 mg
- Potassium: 879 mg
- Phosphorus: 275 mg
- Carbs: 28.6 g
- Protein: 23 g

77. Sirloin Medallions, Green Squash, and Pineapple

Preparation Time: 10 minutes
Cooking Time: 40 minutes
Servings: 4
INGREDIENTS:

- 1 lb. sirloin medallions
- 1 medium baby marrows
- 1 yellow squash
- ½ onion
- 8 oz. pineapple, thinly sliced
- 3 tbsp. olive oil
- 2 tsp. ginger
- ½ tsp. salt
- 1 garlic clove

DIRECTIONS:

1. Retrieve thinly sliced pineapple rings from a can and drain. Set the juice aside.
2. Slice garlic and ginger into fine pieces.
3. Mix the pineapple juice, ginger, garlic, salt, and olive oil in a bowl to create a dressing for the sirloin medallions.
4. Add the sirloin medallions to the marinade and let it sit for 10-15 minutes.
1. Prepare oven to 450°F and line 2 oven trays with parchment paper.
5. Chop the squash into little ½-inch circles and place it on the parchment paper—drizzle 1tbsp. of olive oil on top of it.
6. Cut the onion into small wedges, add to the tray, and drizzle with olive oil.
7. Add pineapple rings next to the squash on the first tray and roast for 6 minutes.
8. Remove the pan and turn the squash and pineapple over. Add the onion onto the tray and roast it for another 5 minutes.
9. Remove sirloin medallions from the marinade. Line another oven tray pan with parchment paper and place the sirloin medallions on top.
10. Cook for 5 minutes and flip the sirloin to cook for another 5 minutes on the other side.
11. Serve the sirloin medallions with the vegetables and pineapple on a platter.

NUTRITION:

- Calories: 264 kcal
- Fat: 12 g
- Carbs: 14 g
- Protein: 25 g
- Sodium: 150 mg
- Potassium: 685 mg
- Phosphorus: 257 mg

78. Chicken and Savory Rice

Preparation Time: 15 minutes
Cooking Time: 45 minutes
Servings: 4
INGREDIENTS:

- 4 medium chicken breasts
- 1 baby marrow, chopped
- 1 red bell pepper, chopped
- 3 tbsp. olive oil
- 1 onion
- 1 garlic clove, minced
- ½ tsp. black pepper
- 1 tbsp. cumin
- ¼ tsp. cayenne pepper
- 2 cups cauliflower rice

DIRECTIONS:

1. Put the 2 tbsp. of olive oil to medium heat and place the chicken breasts into the pan. Cook for 15 minutes and remove from the pan.
2. Add another tbsp. of olive oil to the pan, and add the baby marrow, onion, red pepper, and corn.
3. Sauté the vegetables on medium heat for 10 minutes or until golden brown.
4. Add minced garlic, black pepper, cumin, and cayenne pepper to the vegetables. Stir the vegetables and spices together well.
5. Cut the chicken into a cube and add it back to the pan. Mix it with the vegetables for 5 minutes.
6. In a medium pot, fill it up with water until it is ⅔ full. Add the rice and cook it for 35-40 minutes.
7. Serve the chicken and vegetable mixture on a bed of rice with extra black pepper.

NUTRITION:

- Calories: 374 kcal
- Fat: 6.2 g
- Carbs: 65 g
- Protein: 15 g
- Sodium: 520 mg
- Potassium: 645 mg
- Phosphorus: 268 mg

79. Salmon and Green Beans

Preparation Time: 10 minutes
Cooking Time: 20 minutes
Servings: 4
INGREDIENTS:

- 3 oz. (x 4) salmon fillets
- ½ lb. green beans
- 2 tbsp. dill
- 2 tbsp. coriander
- 2 lemons
- 2 tbsp. olive oil
- 4 tbsp. mayonnaise

DIRECTIONS:

1. Rinse and salmon fillets and wait for them to dry. Don't remove the skin.
2. Wash green beans and chop the tips of the green beans.
3. Heat the oven to 425°F.
4. Spray an oven sheet pan with cooking spray and place the salmon fillets on the sheet pan.
5. Chop up the dill and combine it with the mayonnaise.
6. Put mayo mixture on top of the salmon fillets.
7. Put green beans next to the salmon fillets and drizzle olive oil on top of everything.
8. Place the oven baking sheet in the middle of the oven and cook for 15 minutes.
9. Slice the lemons into wedges and serve with the salmon fillets and green beans.

NUTRITION:

- Calories: 399 kcal
- Fat: 21 g
- Carbs: 8 g
- Protein: 38 g
- Sodium: 229 mg
- Potassium: 1000 mg
- Phosphorus: 723 mg

80. Baked Macaroni and Cheese

Preparation Time: 10 minutes
Cooking Time: 40–45 minutes
Servings: 1
INGREDIENTS:

- 3 cups macaroni
- 2 cups milk
- 2 tbsp. butter, unsalted
- 2 tbsp. all-purpose flour
- 2 ½ cups cheddar
- 2 tbsp. almonds, blanched
- 1 tbsp. thyme
- 1 tbsp. olive oil
- 1 cheese sauce (quick make packets)

DIRECTIONS:

1. Preheat the oven to 350°F.
2. Prepare a medium-sized pot on the stove and fill it up with water.

3. Add the macaroni to the pot with a tbsp. of olive oil for 8-10 minutes. Stir until cooked.
4. In a measuring cup, measure your butter and flour and mix it. Cook in the microwave for 1 minute.
5. Then stir in the milk, spices, and herbs—microwave for 2-3 minutes, or until the mixture is thick.
6. Strain the noodles and add to a casserole dish that has been sprayed with cooking spray, the sauce, and cheese. Mix it well, followed by more cheese on top.
7. Put and bake casserole dish into the oven for 15-20 minutes.
8. Serve with blanched almonds on top.

NUTRITION:

- Calories: 314 kcal
- Fat: 14 g
- Carbs: 34 g
- Protein: 19 g
- Sodium: 373 mg
- Potassium: 120 mg
- Phosphorus: 222 mg

81. Korean Pear Salad

Preparation Time: 5 minutes
Cooking Time: 15 minutes
Servings: 2
INGREDIENTS:

- 6 cups green lettuce
- 4 medium-sized pears, peeled, cored, and diced
- ½ cup sugar
- ½ cup pecan nuts
- ½ cup water
- 2 oz. blue cheese
- ½ cup cranberries
- ½ cup dressing

DIRECTIONS:

1. Dissolve the water and sugar in a frying pan (non-stick).
2. Heat the mixture until it turns into a syrup, and then add the nuts immediately.
3. Place the syrup with the nuts on a piece of parchment paper and separate the nuts while the mixture is hot. Let it cool down.
4. Prepare lettuce in a salad bowl and add the pears, blue cheese, and cranberries to the salad.
5. Add the caramelized nuts to the salad and serve it with a dressing of choice on the side.

NUTRITION:

- Calories: 112 kcal
- Fat: 9 g
- Carbs: 5.5 g

- Protein: 2 g
- Sodium: 130 mg
- Potassium: 160 mg
- Phosphorus: 71.7 mg

82. Beef Enchiladas

Preparation Time: 10 minutes
Cooking Time: 30 minutes
Servings: 1
INGREDIENTS:

- 1 lb. lean beef
- 12 whole-wheat tortillas
- 1 can low-sodium enchilada sauce
- ½ cup onion, diced
- ½ tsp. black pepper
- 1 garlic clove
- 1 tbsp. olive oil
- 1 tsp. cumin

DIRECTIONS:

1. Heat the oven to 375°F.
2. In a medium-sized frying pan, cook the beef in olive oil until completely cooked.
3. Add the minced garlic, diced onion, cumin, and black pepper to the pan and mix everything with the beef.
4. In a separate pan, cook the tortillas in olive oil and dip each cooked tortilla in the enchilada sauce.
5. Fill the tortilla with the meat mixture and roll it up.
6. Bake the tortillas in the pan until crispy, golden brown, and the cheese is melted.

NUTRITION:

- Calories: 177 kcal
- Fat: 6 g
- Carbs: 15 g
- Protein: 15 g
- Sodium: 501 mg
- Potassium: 231 mg
- Phosphorus: 98 mg

83. Chicken and Broccoli Casserole

Preparation Time: 15 minutes
Cooking Time: 45 minutes–1 hour
Servings: 1
INGREDIENTS:

- 2 cups rice, cooked
- 3 chicken breasts
- 2 cups broccoli
- 1 onion, diced
- 2 eggs
- 2 cups cheddar cheese
- 2 tbsp. butter
- 1-2 tbsp. parmesan cheese

DIRECTIONS:

1. Heat the oven to 350°F.
2. Put broccoli in a bowl and cover it with plastic wrap. Microwave the broccoli for 2-3 minutes.
3. Dice the onion and add it with the chicken and the butter in the pan.
4. Cook the chicken for 15 minutes.
5. Once the chicken is cooked, mix it, broccoli, and rice together, and add to a greased casserole dish.
6. Add the grated cheese into the casserole dish and stir well.
7. Put casserole dish in the oven for 30-45 minutes.

NUTRITION:

- Calories: 349 kcal
- Fat: 12 g
- Carbs: 14 g
- Protein: 44 g
- Sodium: 980 mg
- Potassium: 713 mg
- Phosphorus: 451 mg

84. Feta Bean Salad

Preparation Time: 5 minutes
Cooking Time: 20 minutes
Servings: 2
INGREDIENTS:

- 1 tbsp. olive oil
- 2 egg whites, boiled
- 1 cup green beans (8 oz.)
- 1 tbsp. onion
- ½ red chili
- ⅛ cup cilantro
- 1 ½ tbsp. lime juice
- ¼ tbsp. black pepper

DIRECTIONS:

1. Take out the ends of the green beans and cut them into small pieces.
2. Chop the onion, cilantro, and chili and mix it.
3. Use a steamer for cooking green beans for 10 minutes and rinsing with cold water once done.
4. Place all the mixed dry ingredients together in two serving bowls.
5. Chop the egg whites up and place them on top of the salad with crumbled feta.
6. Drizzle a pinch of olive oil with black pepper on top.

NUTRITION:

- Calories: 255 kcal
- Fat: 24 g
- Carbs: 8 g
- Protein: 5 g
- Sodium: 215.6 mg
- Potassium: 211 mg
- Phosphorus: 125 mg

85. Salmon Mayo Sandwich

Preparation Time: 10 minutes
Cooking Time: 20 minutes
Servings: 2
INGREDIENTS:

- 2 salmon fillets
- 2 large slices whole wheat bread
- ½ cup arugula
- ¼ cup peppers, roasted, diced
- 1 tbsp. mayonnaise
- ¼ tsp. lemon-pepper seasoning
- 1-2 tbsp. olive oil
- ¼ tbsp. lime juice

DIRECTIONS:

1. Preheat the pan to medium heat and add olive oil to the pan.
2. Place the salmon fillets in the pan and cover with a lid— Cook the for 10 to 15 minutes.
3. Remove the fillets and place them on foil to cool down for 5-10 minutes. After it's cooled down, remove the skin.
4. Combine a dash of olive oil, lemon-pepper seasoning, and the juice of 1 small lime together.
5. Glaze mixture onto the slices of bread and add it to the pan for 1-2 minutes on each side.
6. Plate the bread with a fresh bed of arugula and salmon on top.

NUTRITION:

- Calories: 255 kcal
- Fat: 24 g
- Carbs: 8 g
- Protein: 5 g
- Sodium: 215.6 mg
- Potassium: 211 mg
- Phosphorus: 125 mg

FISH AND SEAFOOD RECIPES

86.Baked Fish à la Mushrooms

Preparation Time: 10 minutes
Cooking Time: 17 minutes
Servings: 2
INGREDIENTS:

- 1 lb. fresh cod fillet
- 2 tbsp. margarine
- 1-½ cups fresh mushrooms, sliced
- ¼ cup white onion
- 1 tsp. thyme, dried

DIRECTIONS:

1. Prepare fish fillets in a baking dish suitable to fit the Instant Pot.
2. Melt margarine in a pan and add onion and mushroom.
3. Sauté this mixture for 5 minutes, then pours over the fish.
4. Drizzle crushed thyme on top of the sauce.
5. Pour 1 ½ cups water and place a trivet over it.
6. Place the prepared baking dish over this trivet.
7. Cook for 12 minutes on Manual mode at High pressure.
8. Serve warm.

NUTRITION:

- Calories: 155 kcal
- Fat: 7 g
- Carbs: 2 g
- Protein: 21 g
- Sodium: 275 mg
- Potassium: 374 mg
- Phosphorus: 229 mg

87.Shrimp and Asparagus Linguine

Preparation Time: 10 minutes
Cooking Time: 15 minutes
Servings: 4
INGREDIENTS:

- 8 oz. linguini, uncooked
- 1 tbsp. olive oil
- 1-¾ cups asparagus
- ½ cup butter, unsalted
- 2 garlic cloves
- 3 oz. cream cheese
- ¾ tsp. basil, dried
- ⅔ cup dry white wine
- ½ lb. shrimp, peeled, cooked

DIRECTIONS:

1. Prepare and cook the linguini as per the directions on the box and drain.
2. Put asparagus in a steamer basket and drizzle olive over it.
3. Pour 1.5 cup water into the Instant pot and set this basket inside.
4. Seal the lid and cook for 7 minutes on Manual mode at High pressure.
5. Release the pressure, then remove the pot's lid.
6. Slice the asparagus into small pieces.
7. Now melt butter in the Instant pot on sauté mode, after removing the water.
8. Stir in garlic and sauté for 1 minute, then add cream cheese.
9. Cook for 1 minute, then add basil.
10. Continue cooking for 5 minutes, then add white wine. Mix well and add asparagus and shrimp.
11. Toss and serve with cooked pasta.

NUTRITION:

- Calories: 294 kcal
- Fat: 9 g
- Carbs: 25 g
- Protein: 30 g
- Sodium: 389 mg
- Potassium: 464.9 mg
- Phosphorus: 362 mg

88.Old Fashioned Salmon Soup

Preparation Time: 10 minutes
Cooking Time: 12 minutes
Servings: 2
INGREDIENTS:

- 2 tbsp. unsalted butter
- 1 medium carrot, diced
- ½ cup celery, chopped
- ½ cup onion, sliced
- 1 lb. sockeye salmon, cooked, diced
- 2 cups reduced-sodium chicken broth
- 2 cups almond milk
- ⅛ tsp. black pepper
- ¼ cup cornstarch
- ¼ cup water

DIRECTIONS:

1. Dissolve the butter in the Instant Pot on Sauté mode.
2. Add all the veggies and sauté for 5 minutes.
3. Stir in all other ingredients except corn starch and water.
4. Seal the lid and cook for 2 minutes on Manual mode at High pressure.
5. Release the pressure, then remove the pot's lid once the cooking is done.
6. Mix cornstarch with the reserved water and pour it into the soup.
7. Stir cook for 5 minutes on sauté mode until it thickens. Serve warm.

NUTRITION:

- Calories: 223 kcal
- Fat: 1.7 g
- Carbs: 36 g
- Protein: 14 g
- Sodium: 822 mg
- Potassium: 950 mg
- Phosphorus: 82 mg

89.Shrimp in Garlic Sauce

Preparation Time: 10 minutes
Cooking Time: 3 minutes
Servings: 4
INGREDIENTS:

- ½ lb. raw shrimp shelled and deveined
- 8 oz. bowtie pasta, cooked
- 3 tbsp. butter, unsalted
- 3 garlic cloves
- ¼ cup onion
- ½ cup cream cheese, whipped
- ¼ cup half and half cream
- ¼ cup white wine
- 2 tbsp. fresh basil
- ⅛ tsp. black pepper

DIRECTIONS:

1. Dissolve the butter in the Instant Pot on sauté mode.
2. Add onion and garlic to sauté for 1 minute.
3. Toss in the remaining ingredients to the insert.
4. Seal the lid and cook for 2 minutes on Manual mode at High pressure.
5. Serve warm with cooked pasta.

NUTRITION:

- Calories: 336 kcal
- Fat: 13 g
- Carbs: 31.5 g
- Protein: 21 g
- Sodium: 636 mg
- Potassium: 137.5 mg
- Phosphorus: 104 mg

90. Tuna Twist

Preparation Time: 10 minutes
Cooking Time: 30 minutes
Servings: 4

INGREDIENTS:

- 1 can tuna, unsalted or water packaged, drained
- 6 tsp. vinegar
- ½ cup peas, cooked
- ½ cup celery, chopped
- 3 tsp. dill weed, dried
- 12 oz. macaroni, cooked
- ¾ cup mayonnaise

DIRECTIONS:

1. Stir together the macaroni, vinegar, and mayonnaise together until blended and smooth.
2. Stir in the remaining ingredients.
3. Chill before serving.

NUTRITION:

- Calories: 290 kcal
- Fat: 10 g
- Carbs: 32 g
- Protein: 16 g
- Sodium: 307 mg
- Potassium: 175 mg
- Phosphorus: 111 mg

91. Eggplant Seafood Casserole

Preparation Time: 10 minutes
Cooking Time: 20 minutes
Servings: 4

INGREDIENTS:

- 2-medium eggplant, diced
- 1 medium onion, diced
- 1 bell pepper, diced
- ½ cup celery, chopped
- 2 garlic cloves, minced
- ¼ cup olive oil
- ¼ cup lemon juice
- 1 tbsp. Worcestershire sauce
- ¼ tsp. salt-free Creole seasoning
- ½ tsp. hot pepper sauce
- ⅓ cup rice, uncooked
- ¼ cup Parmesan cheese
- 1 dash cayenne pepper
- 3 eggs
- 1 lb. lump crab meat
- ½ lb. shrimp, boiled
- ½ cup breadcrumbs
- 2 tbsp. butter, unsalted, melted

DIRECTIONS:

1. Boil eggplant with water in a saucepan for 5 minutes.
2. Drain the eggplant and keep it aside.
3. Now, sauté the onion with celery, bell pepper, garlic, and oil in the Instant Pot on Sauté mode.
4. Transfer these veggies to the eggplant along with all other ingredients except the breadcrumbs.
5. Mix well, then spread this mixture into a casserole dish suitable to fit in the Instant Pot.
6. Pour 1.5 cup water into the Instant pot and place a trivet over it.
7. Set the casserole dish over the trivet. Spread the crumbs over the casserole.
8. Seal the lid and cook for 15 minutes on Manual mode at High pressure.
9. Remove the pot's lid when done. Serve warm.

NUTRITION:

- Calories: 216 kcal
- Fat: 12 g
- Carbs: 14 g
- Protein: 13 g
- Sodium: 482 mg
- Potassium: 690 mg
- Phosphorus: 182 mg

92. Halibut with Lemon Caper Sauce

Preparation Time: 10 minutes
Cooking Time: 10 minutes
Servings: 4

INGREDIENTS:

- 4 tbsp. lemon juice
- 1 tbsp. olive oil
- 20 oz. raw halibut steaks
- 2 tbsp. butter, unsalted
- 2 tsp. almond flour
- ½ cup chicken broth, reduced-sodium
- ¼ cup white wine
- 1 tsp. capers

- ¼ tsp. white pepper

DIRECTIONS:

1. Season the halibut steaks with 2 tbsp. lemon juice and olive oil in a bowl.
2. Now melt butter in the instant pot on Sauté mode.
3. Stir in the remaining ingredients and whisk well.
4. Place a steamer basket over the sauce mixture and add halibut to the basket.
5. Seal the lid and cook for 5 minutes on Manual mode at High pressure.
6. Once done, release the pressure completely, then remove the pot's lid.
7. Remove the fish and the basket.
8. Add the fish to the sauce and mix well gently. Serve warm.

NUTRITION:

- Calories: 260 kcal
- Fat: 10 g
- Carbs: 5 g
- Protein: 36 g
- Sodium: 118 mg
- Potassium: 573 mg
- Phosphorus: 306 mg

93. Jambalaya

Preparation Time: 10 minutes
Cooking Time: 25 minutes
Servings: 4
INGREDIENTS:

- 2 cups onion
- 1 cup bell pepper
- 2 garlic cloves
- 2 cups converted white rice, uncooked
- ½ tsp. black pepper
- 8 oz. low-sodium tomato sauce, canned
- 2 cups low-sodium beef broth
- 2 lb. raw shrimp
- ½ cup margarine

DIRECTIONS:

1. Toss all the ingredients except margarine in a baking dish.
2. Place the margarine slice on top of the mixture.
3. Cover the dish with aluminum foil.
4. Pour 1.5 cups over into the instant pot and set the trivet over it.
5. Place the prepared baking dish over the trivet.
6. Press manual mode at high pressure and seal the lid— Cook for 25 minutes.
7. Once done, release the pressure and gently remove the pot's lid. Serve warm.

NUTRITION:

- Calories: 207 kcal
- Fat: 4 g
- Carbs: 30 g
- Protein: 12 g
- Sodium: 462 mg
- Potassium: 304 mg
- Phosphorus: 107 mg

94. Shrimp Szechuan

Preparation Time: 10 minutes
Cooking Time: 9 minutes
Servings: 4
INGREDIENTS:

- 1 tbsp. canola oil
- ½ cup bean sprouts
- ½ cup green bell pepper, chopped
- ½ cup onion, chopped
- ½ cup raw mushroom pieces
- 1 tsp. ginger root, grated
- ½ tsp. garlic powder
- 1 tbsp. sesame oil
- 1 tsp. red pepper flakes
- ⅓ cup low-sodium chicken broth
- 4 tbsp. sherry wine
- 1 tsp. cornstarch
- 4 oz. shrimp, frozen

DIRECTIONS:

1. Start by heating oil in the Instant pot on Sauté mode.
2. Toss in onions, ginger, mushrooms, bell pepper, and bean sprouts.
3. Sauté for 2 minutes, then toss in all the ingredients except cornstarch.
4. Seal the lid and cook for 2 minutes on Manual mode at High pressure.
5. Release the pressure completely, then remove the pot's lid once done cooking.
6. Put and mix the cornstarch with 2 tbsp. of water in a bowl.
7. Pour this mixture into the Instant pot and cook for 5 minutes on sauté mode. Serve warm.

NUTRITION:

- Calories: 140 kcal
- Fat: 4.3 g
- Carbs: 6 g
- Protein: 19 g
- Sodium: 372 mg
- Potassium: 204.3 mg
- Phosphorus: 196 mg

95. Shrimp Scampi Linguine

Preparation Time: 15 minutes
Cooking Time: 15 minutes
Servings: 4
INGREDIENTS:

- 4 oz. linguine, uncooked
- 1 tsp. olive oil
- 2 tsp. garlic, minced
- 4 oz. shrimp, peeled and chopped
- ½ cup dry white wine
- juice of 1 lemon
- 1 tbsp. fresh basil, chopped
- ½ cup heavy whipping cream
- Black pepper, ground

DIRECTIONS:

1. Cook the linguine based on the package instructions.
2. Warm olive oil in a skillet.
3. Sauté the garlic and shrimp for 6 minutes or until the shrimp is opaque and just cooked through.
4. Add the lemon juice, wine, and basil. Cook for 5 minutes.
5. Stir in the cream and simmer for 2 minutes more.
6. Add the linguine to the skillet and toss to coat.
7. Divide the pasta onto 4 plates to serve.

NUTRITION:

- Calories: 219 kcal
- Fat: 7 g
- Carb: 21 g
- Protein: 12 g
- Sodium: 42 mg
- Potassium: 155 mg
- Phosphorus: 119 mg

96. Grilled Shrimp with Cucumber Lime Salsa

Preparation Time: 15 minutes
Cooking Time: 10 minutes
Servings: 4
INGREDIENTS:

- 2 tbsp. olive oil
- 6 oz. shrimp, peeled and deveined, tails left on large
- 1 tsp. garlic, minced
- ½ cup English cucumber, chopped
- ½ cup mango, chopped
- Zest of 1 lime
- Juice of 1 lime
- Black pepper, ground
- Lime wedges, for garnish

DIRECTIONS:

1. Soak 4 skewers in water for 30 minutes.
2. Preheat the barbecue to medium heat.
3. In a bowl, toss together the olive oil, shrimp, and garlic.
4. Thread the shrimp onto the skewers, about 4 shrimp per skewer.
5. In a bowl, stir together the mango, cucumber, lime zest, and lime juice and season the salsa lightly with pepper. Set aside.
6. Grill the shrimp for 10 minutes, turning once or until the shrimp is opaque and cooked through.
7. Season the shrimp lightly with pepper.
8. Serve the shrimp on the cucumber salsa with lime wedges on the side.

NUTRITION:

- Calories: 120 kcal
- Fat: 8 g
- Carb: 4 g
- Protein: 9 g
- Sodium: 60 mg
- Potassium: 129 mg
- Phosphorus: 91 mg

97. Crab Cakes with Lime Salsa

Preparation Time: 20 minutes
Cooking Time: 20 minutes
Servings: 4
INGREDIENTS:

For the Salsa:

- ½ English cucumber, diced
- 1 Lime, chopped
- ½ cup red bell pepper, boiled and chopped
- 1 tsp. fresh cilantro, hopped
- Black pepper, ground

For the crab cakes:

- 8 oz. Queen crab meat
- ¼ cup Breadcrumbs
- 1 Small egg
- ¼ cup red bell pepper, boiled and chopped
- 1 Scallion, both green and white parts, minced
- 1 tbsp. fresh parsley, chopped
- Splash hot sauce
- Olive oil spray, for the pan

DIRECTIONS:

1. Combine the lime, cucumber, red pepper, and cilantro in a small bowl to make the salsa. Season with pepper and set aside.
2. To make the crab cakes, mix the breadcrumbs, crab, red pepper, egg, scallion, parsley, and hot sauce until it holds together in a bowl. Add more if necessary.
3. Form the crab mixture into 4 patties.
4. Refrigerate for 1 hour to firm them.
5. Place the skillet on medium heat and spray with olive oil.
6. Cook the crab cakes in batches, turning, for about 5 minutes per side or until golden brown.
7. Serve the crab cakes with salsa.

NUTRITION:

- Calories: 115 kcal
- Fat: 2 g
- Carb: 7 g
- Protein: 16 g
- Sodium: 421 mg
- Potassium: 200 mg
- Phosphorus: 110 mg

98.Sweet Glazed Salmon

Preparation Time: 10 minutes
Cooking Time: 10 minutes
Servings: 4
INGREDIENTS:

- 2 tbsp. honey
- 1 tsp. lemon zest
- ½ tsp. black pepper, ground
- 4 (3-oz.) each salmon fillets
- 1 tbsp. olive oil
- ½ scallion, white and green parts, chopped

DIRECTIONS:

1. In a bowl, stir together the lemon zest, honey, and pepper.
2. Clean salmon and pat dry with paper towels.
3. Rub the honey mixture all over each fillet.
4. Prepare a skillet, heat the olive oil.
5. Add the salmon fillets and cook the salmon for 10 minutes, turning once.
6. Serve topped with chopped scallion.

NUTRITION:

- Calories: 240 kcal
- Fat: 15 g
- Carb: 9 g
- Protein: 17 g
- Sodium: 51 mg
- Potassium: 317 mg
- Phosphorus: 205 mg

99.Herb-Crusted Baked Haddock

Preparation Time: 10 minutes
Cooking Time: 20 minutes
Servings: 4
INGREDIENTS:

- ½ cup breadcrumbs
- 3 tbsp. fresh parsley, chopped
- 1 tbsp. lemon zest
- 1 tsp. fresh thyme, chopped
- ¼ tsp. black pepper, ground
- 1 tbsp. butter, melted and unsalted
- 12-oz. haddock fillets, deboned and skinned

DIRECTIONS:

1. Preheat the oven to 350°F.
2. In a bowl, mix the parsley, breadcrumbs, lemon zest, thyme, and pepper until well combined.
3. Add the melted butter and toss until the mixture resembles coarse crumbs.
4. Place the haddock on a baking sheet and spoon the bread crumb mixture on top, pressing down firmly.
5. Bake the haddock in the oven for 20 minutes or until the fish is just cooked through and flakes off in chunks when pressed.

NUTRITION:

- Calories: 143 kcal
- Fat: 4 g
- Carb: 10 g
- Protein: 16 g
- Sodium: 281 mg
- Potassium: 285 mg
- Phosphorus: 216 mg

100. Baked Cod with Salsa

Preparation Time: 20 minutes
Cooking Time: 10 minutes
Servings: 4
INGREDIENTS:

For the salsa:

- ½ English cucumber, chopped
- 2 tbsp. fresh dill, chopped
- Juice of 1 lime
- Zest of 1 lime
- ¼ cup red bell pepper, boiled and minced
- ½ tsp. sugar, granulated

For the fish:

- 12 oz. Cod fillets, deboned and cut into 4 servings
- Juice of 1 lemon
- ½ tsp. black pepper, ground
- 1 tsp. olive oil

DIRECTIONS:

1. To make the cucumber salsa: mix the salsa ingredients in a bowl and set aside.
2. To make the fish: preheat the oven to 350°F.
3. Put the fish on a pie plate and add the lemon juice over the fillets.
4. Sprinkle with pepper and drizzle the olive oil evenly over the fillets.
5. Bake the fish for 6 minutes or until it flakes easily with a fork.
6. Transfer the fish to 4 plates and serve topped with cucumber salsa.

NUTRITION:

- Calories: 110 kcal
- Fat: 2 g
- Carb: 3 g
- Protein: 20 g
- Sodium: 67 mg
- Potassium: 275 mg
- Phosphorus: 120 mg

101. Cilantro-Lime Flounder

Preparation Time: 20 minutes
Cooking Time: 5 minutes
Servings: 4
INGREDIENTS:

- ¼ cup Homemade mayonnaise
- Juice of 1 lime
- Zest of 1 lime
- ½ cup fresh cilantro, chopped
- 4 (3-oz.) flounder fillets
- Black pepper, ground

DIRECTIONS:

1. Preheat the oven to 400°F.
2. In a bowl, stir together the cilantro, lime juice, lime zest, and mayonnaise.
3. Place 4 pieces of foil, about 8 by 8 inches square, on a clean work surface.
4. Place a flounder fillet in the center of each square.
5. Top the fillets evenly with the mayonnaise mixture.
6. Season the flounder with pepper.
7. Fold the foil's sides over the fish, create a snug packet, and place the foil packets on a baking sheet.
8. Bake the fish for 5 minutes.
9. Unfold the packets and serve.

NUTRITION:

- Calories: 92 kcal
- Fat: 4 g
- Carb: 2 g
- Protein: 12 g
- Sodium: 267 mg
- Potassium: 137 mg
- Phosphorus: 208 mg

102. Cooked Tilapia with Mango Salsa

Preparation Time: 2 hours
Cooking Time: 10 minutes
Servings: 2
INGREDIENTS:

- 2 (3 oz. each) fresh tilapia fillets
- ½ red onion, diced
- ½ red bell pepper, diced
- 2 tbsp. fresh cilantro
- ¼ cup Olive oil
- 1 tsp. Black pepper
- 1 Lime
- 4 Crackers/slices of melba toast

DIRECTIONS:

1. Preheat the broiler on medium heat.
2. Cut tilapia into small bite-size pieces.
3. Place tilapia under the broiler for 7 to 10 minutes or until cooked through.
4. Remove and allow to cool in a bowl. Squeeze the juice from the lime on the top and mix well.
5. Mix the onion, bell pepper, cilantro, mango, pepper, and oil with the cooked tilapia and marinate for 2 hours in the refrigerator.
6. Divide into 2 bowls and serve with crackers.

NUTRITION:

- Calories: 389 kcal
- Fat: 29 g
- Carb: 18 g
- Protein: 17 g
- Sodium: 134 mg
- Potassium: 217 mg
- Phosphorus: 183 mg

103. Cilantro and Chili Infused Swordfish

Preparation Time: 30 minutes
Cooking Time: 15 minutes
Servings: 2
INGREDIENTS:

- 2 (30 oz.) Swordfish fillets
- 4 tsp. fresh cilantro
- 1 onion, finely diced
- 1 tsp. brown sugar
- 1 red chili, diced
- 1 lemon
- 1 tbsp. extra virgin olive oil
- 1 garlic clove, minced

DIRECTIONS:

1. Soak vegetables in warm water.
2. Meanwhile, add fish to an ovenproof baking dish.
3. Whisk onion, cilantro, chili, sugar, lemon juice, oil, and garlic in another bowl.
4. Pour the marinade over the swordfish and turn the fish over to coat both sides.
5. Marinate in the refrigerator for 30 minutes or more.
6. Preheat the broiler to medium heat.
7. Place oven dish under the broiler for 6 to 7 minutes on each side or until fish flakes easily with a fork. Serve hot.

NUTRITION:

- Calories: 340 kcal
- Fat: 16 g
- Carb: 25 g
- Protein: 23 g
- Sodium: 258 mg
- Potassium: 243 mg
- Phosphorus: 284 mg

104. Citrus Tuna Ceviche

Preparation Time: 5 minutes
Cooking Time: 0 minutes
Servings: 2
INGREDIENTS:

- 1 (5 oz.) low-sodium tuna, drained and rinsed, water-packed
- 1 tbsp. cilantro
- ½ red onion, diced
- 1 tsp. black pepper
- 1 lemon
- 1 tsp. red wine vinegar
- 1 red bell pepper, chopped

DIRECTIONS:

1. Add tuna together with the ingredients into a serving bowl, mix well, and cover plastic wrap.
2. Marinate as long as possible.
3. Serve with a salad or sandwich.

NUTRITION:

- Calories: 127 kcal
- Fat: 1 g
- Carbs: 10 g
- Protein: 21 g
- Sodium: 278 mg
- Potassium: 149 mg
- Phosphorus: 116 mg

105. <u>Baked Trout</u>

Preparation Time: 5 minutes
Cooking Time: 10 minutes
Servings: 8
INGREDIENTS:

- 2-lb. trout fillet
- 1 tbsp. oil
- 1 tsp. salt-free lemon pepper
- ½ tsp. paprika

DIRECTIONS:

1. Prepare oven to 350°F.
2. Coat fillet with oil.
3. Place fish on a baking pan.
4. Season with lemon pepper and paprika.
5. Bake for 10 minutes.

NUTRITION:

- Calories: 161 kcal
- Protein: 21 g
- Carbohydrates: 0 g
- Fat: 8 g
- Potassium: 385 mg
- Sodium: 109 mg
- Phosphorus: 227 mg

106. <u>Curried Fish Cakes</u>

Preparation Time: 10 minutes
Cooking Time: 18 minutes
Servings: 4
INGREDIENTS:

- ¾ lb. Atlantic cod, cubed
- 1 apple, peeled and cubed
- 1 tbsp. yellow curry paste
- 2 tbsp. cornstarch
- 1 tbsp. ginger root, peeled, grated
- 1 large egg
- 1 tbsp. lemon juice, freshly squeezed
- ⅛ tsp. black pepper, freshly ground
- ½ cup puffed rice cereal, crushed
- 1 tbsp. olive oil

DIRECTIONS:

1. Put the cod, apple, curry, cornstarch, ginger, egg, lemon juice, and pepper in a blender or food processor. Process until finely chopped. Avoid over-processing, or the mixture will become mushy.
2. Place the rice cereal on a shallow plate.
3. Form the mixture into 8 patties.
4. Dredge the patties in the rice cereal to coat.
5. Cook patties for 3 to 5 minutes per side, turning once until a meat thermometer registers 160°f.
6. Serve.

NUTRITION:

- Calories: 188 kcal
- Fat: 6 g
- Carbohydrates: 12 g
- Protein: 21 g
- Sodium: 150 mg
- Potassium: 292 mg
- Phosphorus: 150 mg

VEGETARIAN AND VEGAN RECIPES

107. Sautéed Green Beans

Preparation Time: 10 minutes
Cooking Time: 15 minutes
Servings: 4
INGREDIENTS:

- 2 cup green beans, frozen
- ½ cup red bell pepper
- 4 tsp. margarine
- ¼ cup onion
- 1 tsp. dill weed, dried
- 1 tsp. parsley, dried
- ¼ tsp. black pepper

DIRECTIONS:

1. Cook green beans in a large pan of boiling water until tender, then drain.
2. While the beans are cooking, melt the margarine in a skillet and fry the other vegetables.
3. Add the beans to sautéed vegetables.
4. Sprinkle with freshly ground pepper and serve with meat and fish dishes.

NUTRITION:

- Calories: 67 kcal
- Carbs: 8 g
- Protein: 4 g
- Sodium: 5 mg
- Potassium: 179 mg
- Phosphorous: 32 mg

108. Garlicky Penne Pasta with Asparagus

Preparation Time: 10 minutes
Cooking Time: 10 minutes
Servings: 4

INGREDIENTS:

- 2 tbsp. butter
- 1 lb. asparagus, cut into 2-inch pieces
- 2 tsp. lemon juice
- 4 cup whole wheat penne pasta, cooked
- ¼ cup Parmesan cheese, shredded
- ¼ tsp. Tabasco® hot sauce

DIRECTIONS:

1. Add olive oil and butter in a skillet over medium heat.
2. Fry garlic and red pepper flakes for 2-3 minutes.
3. Add asparagus, Tabasco sauce, lemon juice, and black pepper to skillet and cook for a further 6 minutes.
4. Add hot pasta and cheese. Toss and serve.

NUTRITION:

- Calories: 387 kcal
- Carbs: 49 g
- Protein: 13 g
- Sodium: 93 mg
- Potassium: 258 mg
- Phosphorous: 252 mg

109. Garlic Mashed Potatoes

Preparation Time: 5 minutes
Cooking Time: 20 minutes
Servings: 4
INGREDIENTS:

- 2 medium potatoes, peeled and sliced
- ¼ cup butter
- ¼ cup 1% low-fat milk
- 2 garlic cloves

DIRECTIONS:

1. Double-boil or soak the potatoes to reduce potassium if you are on a low potassium diet.
2. Boil potatoes and garlic until soft. Drain.
3. Beat the potatoes and garlic with butter and milk until smooth.

NUTRITION:

- Calories: 168 kcal
- Carbs: 29 g
- Protein: 5 g
- Sodium: 59 mg
- Potassium: 161 g
- Phosphorous: 57 mg

110. Ginger Glazed Carrots

Preparation Time: 10 minutes
Cooking Time: 20 minutes
Servings: 4
INGREDIENTS:

- 2 cups carrots, sliced into 1-inch pieces
- ¼ cup apple juice
- 2 tbsp. margarine, melted
- ¼ cup boiling water
- 1 tbsp. sugar
- 1 tsp. cornstarch
- ¼ tsp. salt
- ¼ tsp. ginger, ground

DIRECTIONS:

1. Cook carrots until tender.
2. Mix sugar, cornstarch, salt, ginger, apple juice, and margarine together
3. Pour mixture over carrots and cook for 10 minutes until thickened.

NUTRITION:

- Calories: 101 kcal
- Fat: 3 g
- Carbs: 14 g
- Protein: 1 g
- Sodium: 87 mg
- Potassium: 202 g
- Phosphorous: 26 mg

111. Carrot-Apple Casserole

Preparation Time: 15 minutes
Cooking Time: 50 minutes
Servings: 8
INGREDIENTS:

- 6 large carrots, peeled and sliced
- 4 large apples, peeled and sliced
- 3 tbsp. butter
- ½ cup apple juice
- 5 tbsp. all-purpose flour
- 2 tbsp. brown sugar
- ½ tsp. nutmeg, ground

DIRECTIONS:

1. Preheat oven to 350°F.
2. Let the carrots boil for 5 minutes or until tender. Drain.
3. Arrange the carrots and apples in a large casserole dish.
4. Mix the flour, brown sugar, and nutmeg in a small bowl.
5. Rub in butter to make a crumb topping.
6. Sprinkle the crumb over the carrots and apples, then drizzle with juice.
7. Bake until bubbling and golden brown.

NUTRITION:

- Calories: 245 kcal
- Fat: 6 g
- Carbs: 49 g
- Protein: 1 g
- Sodium: 91 mg
- Potassium: 169 mg
- Phosphorous: 17 mg

112. Creamy Shells with Peas

Preparation Time: 15 minutes
Cooking Time: 15 minutes
Servings: 4
INGREDIENTS:

- 1 cup part-skim ricotta cheese
- ½ cup Parmesan cheese, grated
- 1 cup onion, chopped
- ¾ cup green peas, frozen
- 1 tbsp. olive oil
- ¼ tsp. black pepper
- 3 garlic cloves, minced
- 3 cup whole-wheat small shell pasta, cooked
- 1 tbsp. lemon juice
- 2 tbsp. butter, unsalted

DIRECTIONS:

1. Place ricotta, Parmesan cheese, butter, and pepper in a large bowl.
2. Add the garlic and onion to the same skillet and fry until soft. Add to bowl with ricotta.
3. Cook the peas and add to the ricotta.
4. Add half a cup of the reserved cooking water and lemon juice to the ricotta mixture and mix well.
5. Add the pasta, and peas to the bowl and mix well.
6. Put freshly ground black pepper and serve.

NUTRITION:

- Calories: 429 kcal
- Fat: 14 g
- Carbs: 27 g
- Protein: 13 g
- Sodium: 244 mg
- Potassium: 172 mg
- Phosphorous: 203 mg

113. Double-Boiled Stewed Potatoes

Preparation Time: 20 minutes
Cooking Time: 30 minutes
Servings: 4
INGREDIENTS:

- 2 cup potatoes, diced into ½-inch cubes
- ½ cup hot water
- ½ cup liquid non-dairy creamer
- ¼ tsp. garlic powder
- ¼ tsp. black pepper
- 2 tbsp. margarine
- 2 tsp. all-purpose white flour

DIRECTIONS:

1. Soak or double boil the potatoes if you are on a low potassium diet.
2. Boil potatoes for 15 minutes.
3. Drain potatoes and return to pan. Add half a cup of hot water, creamer, garlic powder, pepper, and margarine. Heat to a boil.

4. Mix the flour with a tbsp. of water and then stir this into the potatoes. Cook for 3 minutes until the mixture has thickened and the flour has cooked.

NUTRITION:

- Calories: 184 kcal
- Carbs: 25 g
- Protein: 2 g
- Potassium: 161 mg
- Phosphorous: 65 mg

114. Double-Boiled Country Style Fried Potatoes

Preparation Time: 20 minutes
Cooking Time: 20 minutes
Servings: 4
INGREDIENTS:

- 2 medium potatoes, cut into large chips
- ½ cup canola oil
- ¼ tsp. ground cumin
- ¼ tsp. paprika
- ¼ tsp. white pepper
- 3 tbsp. ketchup

DIRECTIONS:

1. Soak or double boil the potatoes if you are on a low potassium diet.
2. Warm oil in a skillet with medium heat.
3. Fry the potatoes for around 10 minutes until golden brown.
4. Drain potatoes, then sprinkle with cumin, pepper, and paprika.
5. Serve with ketchup or mayo.

NUTRITION:

- Calories: 156 kcal
- Fat: 0.1 g
- Carbs: 21 g
- Protein: 2 g
- Sodium: 3 mg
- Potassium: 296 mg
- Phosphorous: 34 mg

115. Broccoli-Onion Latkes

Preparation Time: 15 minutes
Cooking Time: 20 minutes
Servings: 4
INGREDIENTS:

- 3 cups broccoli florets, diced
- ½ cup onion, chopped
- 2 large eggs, beaten
- 2 tbsp. all-purpose white flour
- 2 tbsp. olive oil

DIRECTIONS:

1. Cook the broccoli for around 5 minutes until tender. Drain.
2. Mix the flour into the eggs.
3. Combine the onion, broccoli, and egg mixture and stir through.
4. Prepare olive oil in a skillet on medium-high heat.
5. Drop a spoon of the mixture onto the pan to make 4 latkes.
6. Cook each side until golden brown.
7. Tap on a paper towel and serve.

NUTRITION:

- Calories: 140 kcal
- Fat Carbs: 7 g
- Protein: 6 g
- Sodium: 58 mg
- Potassium: 276 mg
- Phosphorous: 101 mg

116. Cranberry Cabbage

Preparation Time: 10 minutes
Cooking Time: 20 minutes
Servings: 8
INGREDIENTS:

- 10 oz. whole-berry cranberry sauce, canned
- 1 tbsp. fresh lemon juice
- 1 medium head red cabbage
- ¼ tsp. cloves, ground

DIRECTIONS:

1. Place the cranberry sauce, lemon juice, and cloves in a large pan and bring to a boil.
2. Add the cabbage and reduce it to a simmer.
3. Cook until the cabbage is tender, occasionally stirring to make sure the sauce does not stick.
4. Deliciously serve with beef, lamb, or pork.

NUTRITION:

- Calories: 73 kcal
- Fat: 0 g
- Carbs: 18 g
- Protein: 1 g
- Sodium: 32 mg
- Potassium: 138 mg
- Phosphorous: 18 mg

117. Cauliflower Rice

Preparation Time: 5 minutes
Cooking Time: 10 minutes
Servings: 1
INGREDIENTS:

- 1 small head cauliflower cut into florets
- 1 tbsp. butter
- ¼ tsp. black pepper
- ¼ tsp. garlic powder
- ¼ tsp. salt-free herb seasoning blend

DIRECTIONS:

1. Blitz cauliflower pieces in a food processor until it has a grain-like consistency.
2. Melt butter in a saucepan and add spices.
3. Add the cauliflower rice grains and cook over low-medium heat for approximately 10 minutes.
4. Serve as an alternative to rice with curries, stews, and starch to accompany meat and fish dishes.

NUTRITION:

- Calories: 47 kcal
- Fat Carbs: 4 g
- Protein: 1 g
- Sodium: 300 mg
- Potassium: 206 mg
- Phosphorous: 31 mg

118. Spicy Mushroom Stir-Fry

Preparation Time: 10 minutes
Cooking Time: 10 minutes
Servings: 4
INGREDIENTS:

- 1 cup low-sodium vegetable broth
- 2 tbsp. cornstarch
- 1 tsp. low-sodium soy sauce
- ½ tsp. ginger, ground
- ⅛ tsp. cayenne pepper
- 2 tbsp. olive oil
- 2 (8-oz.) packages mushrooms, sliced button
- 1 red bell pepper, chopped
- 1 jalapeño pepper, minced
- 3 cups cauliflower rice that has been cooked in unsalted water
- 2 tbsp. sesame oil

DIRECTIONS:

1. Get a small bowl, mix together the broth, cornstarch, soy sauce, ginger, and cayenne pepper, and set aside.
2. Warm olive oil in a wok or heavy skillet over high heat.
3. Add the mushrooms and peppers and stir-fry for 3 to 5 minutes or until the vegetables are tender-crisp.
4. Stir broth mixture and add it to the wok; stir-fry until the vegetables are tender and the sauce thickens.
5. Serve the stir-fry over the hot cooked cauliflower rice and drizzle with the sesame oil.

NUTRITION:

- Calories: 361 kcal
- Fat: 16 g
- Carbohydrates: 49 g
- Protein: 8 g
- Sodium: 95 mg
- Phosphorus: 267 mg
- Potassium: 582 mg

119. Curried Veggies and Rice

Preparation Time: 12 minutes
Cooking Time: 18 minutes
Servings: 4
INGREDIENTS:

- ¼ cup olive oil
- 1 cup long-grain white basmati rice
- 4 garlic cloves, minced
- 2 ½ tsp. curry powder
- ½ cup shiitake mushrooms, sliced
- 1 red bell pepper, chopped
- 1 cup edamame, frozen, shelled
- 2 cups low-sodium vegetable broth
- ⅛ tsp. black pepper, freshly ground

DIRECTIONS:

1. Warm olive oil on medium heat.
2. Add the rice, garlic, curry powder, mushrooms, bell pepper, and edamame; cook, stirring, for 2 minutes.
3. Add the broth and black pepper and bring to a boil.
4. Reduce the heat to low, partially cover the pot, and simmer for 15 to 18 minutes or until the rice is tender. Stir and serve.

NUTRITION:

- Calories: 347 kcal
- Fat: 16 g
- Carbohydrates: 44 g
- Protein: 8 g
- Sodium: 114 mg
- Phosphorus: 131 mg
- Potassium: 334 mg

120. Spicy Veggie Pancakes

Preparation Time: 10 minutes
Cooking Time: 10 minutes
Servings: 4
INGREDIENTS:

- 3 tbsp. olive oil, divided
- 2 small onions, finely chopped
- 1 jalapeño pepper, minced
- ¾ cup carrot, grated
- ¾ cup cabbage, finely chopped
- 1½ cups quick-cooking oats
- ¾ cup brown rice, cooked
- ¾ cup water
- ½ cup whole-wheat flour
- 1 large egg
- 1 large egg white

- 1 tsp. baking soda
- ¼ tsp. cayenne pepper

DIRECTIONS:

1. In a skillet, heat 2 tsp. oil over medium heat.
2. Sauté the onion, jalapeño, carrot, and cabbage for 4 minutes.
3. In the meantime, combine the oats, rice, water, flour, egg, egg white, baking soda, and cayenne pepper in a medium bowl until well mixed.
4. Put the cooked vegetables into the mixture and stir to combine.
5. Add and warm the remaining oil in a large skillet over medium heat.
6. Drop the mixture into the skillet, about ⅓ cup per pancake. Cook until bubbles form on the pancakes' surface and the edges look cooked, then carefully flip them over.
7. Repeat with the remaining mixture and serve.

NUTRITION:

- Calories: 323 kcal
- Fat: 11 g
- Carbohydrates: 48 g
- Protein: 10 g
- Sodium: 366 mg
- Potassium: 381 mg
- Phosphorus: 263 mg

121. Egg and Veggie Fajitas

Preparation Time: 15 minutes
Cooking Time: 10 minutes
Servings: 4
INGREDIENTS:

- 3 large eggs
- 3 egg whites
- 2 tsp. chili powder
- 1 tbsp. butter, unsalted
- 1 onion, chopped
- 2 garlic cloves, minced
- 1 jalapeño pepper, minced

- 1 red bell pepper, chopped
- 1 cup corn, frozen, thawed and drained
- 8 (6-inch) corn tortillas

DIRECTIONS:

1. Whisk the eggs, egg whites, and chili powder in a small bowl until well combined. Set aside.
2. Prepare a large skillet and melt the butter on medium heat.
3. Sauté the onion, garlic, jalapeño, bell pepper, and corn until the vegetables are tender, 3 to 4 minutes.
4. Put the beaten egg mixture into the skillet. Cook, occasionally stirring, until the eggs form large curds and are set, 3 to 5 minutes.
5. Meanwhile, soften the corn tortillas as directed on the package.
6. Divide the egg mixture among the softened corn tortillas. Roll the tortillas up and serve.

NUTRITION:

- Calories: 316 kcal
- Fat: 14 g
- Carbohydrates: 35 g
- Protein: 14 g
- Sodium: 167 mg
- Potassium: 408 mg
- Phosphorus: 287 mg

122. Vegetable Biryani

Preparation Time: 10 minutes
Cooking Time: 15 minutes
Servings: 4
INGREDIENTS:

- 2 tbsp. olive oil
- 1 onion, diced
- 4 garlic cloves, minced
- 1 tbsp. fresh ginger root, peeled and grated
- 1 cup carrot, grated
- 2 cups cauliflower, chopped
- 1 cup baby peas, thawed, frozen
- 2 tsp. curry powder
- 1 cup low-sodium vegetable broth
- 3 cups brown rice, frozen, cooked

DIRECTIONS:

1. Get a skillet and heat the olive oil on medium heat.
2. Add onion, garlic, and ginger root. Sauté, frequently stirring, until tender-crisp, 2 minutes.
3. Add the carrot, cauliflower, peas, and curry powder and cook for 2 minutes longer.

4. Put vegetable broth. Cover the skillet partially, and simmer on low for 6 to 7 minutes or until the vegetables are tender.
5. Meanwhile, heat the rice as directed on the package.
6. Stir the rice into the vegetable mixture and serve.

NUTRITION:

- Calories: 378 kcal
- Fat: 16 g
- Carbohydrates: 53 g
- Protein: 8 g
- Sodium: 113 mg
- Potassium: 510 mg
- Phosphorus: 236 mg

123.   Pesto Pasta Salad

Preparation Time: 15 minutes
Cooking Time: 15 minutes
Servings: 4
INGREDIENTS:

- 1 cup fresh basil leaves
- ½ cup fresh parsley leaves, packed
- ½ cup arugula, chopped
- 2 tbsp. Parmesan cheese, grated
- ¼ cup extra-virgin olive oil
- 3 tbsp. mayonnaise
- 2 tbsp. water
- 12 oz. whole-wheat rotini pasta
- 1 red bell pepper, chopped
- 1 medium yellow summer squash, sliced
- 1 cup baby peas, frozen

DIRECTIONS:

1. Boil water in a large pot.
2. Meanwhile, combine the basil, parsley, arugula, cheese, and olive oil in a blender or food processor. Process until the herbs are finely chopped. Add the mayonnaise and water, then process again. Set aside.

3. Prepare the pasta to the pot of boiling water; cook according to package directions, about 8 to 9 minutes. Strain well, reserving ¼ cup of the cooking liquid.
4. Combine the pesto, pasta, bell pepper, squash, and peas in a large bowl and toss gently, adding enough reserved pasta cooking liquid to make a sauce on the salad. Serve immediately or cover and chill, then serve.
5. Keep with cover in the refrigerator for up to 3 days.

NUTRITION:

- Calories: 378 kcal
- Fat: 24 g
- Carbohydrates: 35 g
- Protein: 9 g
- Sodium: 163 mg
- Potassium: 472 mg
- Phosphorus: 213 mg

124.   Barley Blueberry Avocado Salad

Preparation Time: 15 minutes
Cooking Time: 15 minutes
Servings: 4
INGREDIENTS:

- 1 cup quick-cooking barley
- 3 cups low-sodium vegetable broth
- 3 tbsp. extra-virgin olive oil
- 2 tbsp. lemon juice, freshly squeezed
- 1 tsp. yellow mustard
- 1 tsp. honey
- ½ avocado, peeled and chopped
- 2 cups blueberries
- ¼ cup feta cheese, crumbled

DIRECTIONS:

1. Combine the barley and vegetable broth in a medium saucepan and bring to a simmer.
2. Lower heat to low, partially cover the pan, and simmer for 10 to 12 minutes or until the barley is tender.
3. Meanwhile, stir together the olive oil, lemon juice, mustard, and honey in a serving bowl until blended.
4. Drain the barley if necessary and add to the bowl; toss to combine.

5. Add the avocado, blueberries, and feta and toss gently. Serve.

NUTRITION:

- Calories: 345 kcal
- Fat: 16 g
- Carbohydrates: 44 g
- Protein: 7 g
- Sodium: 259 mg
- Potassium: 301 mg
- Phosphorus: 152 mg

125. Pasta with Creamy Broccoli Sauce

Preparation Time: 15 minutes
Cooking Time: 15 minutes
Servings: 4
INGREDIENTS:

- 2 tbsp. olive oil
- 1-lb. broccoli florets
- 3 garlic cloves, halved
- 1 cup low-sodium vegetable broth
- ½-lb. whole-wheat spaghetti pasta
- 4 oz. cream cheese
- 1 tsp. basil leaves, dried
- ½ cup Parmesan cheese, grated

DIRECTIONS:

1. Prepare a large pot of water to a boil.
2. Put olive oil in a large skillet. Sauté the broccoli and garlic for 3 minutes.
3. Add the broth to the skillet and bring it to a simmer. Change the heat to low, partially cover the skillet, and simmer until the broccoli is tender about 5 to 6 minutes.
4. Cook the pasta based on the package directions. Drain when al dente, reserving 1 cup pasta water.
5. When the broccoli is tender, add the cream cheese and basil—purée using an immersion blender.
6. Put mixture into a food processor, about half at a time, and purée until smooth and transfer the sauce back into the skillet.
7. Add the cooked pasta to the broccoli sauce. Toss, adding enough pasta water until the sauce coats the pasta completely. Sprinkle with the Parmesan and serve.

NUTRITION:

- Calories: 302 kcal
- Fat: 14 g
- Carbohydrates: 36 g
- Protein: 11 g
- Sodium: 260 mg
- Potassium: 375 mg
- Phosphorus: 223 mg

126. Asparagus Fried Rice

Preparation Time: 10 minutes
Cooking Time: 10 minutes
Servings: 1
INGREDIENTS:

- 3 large eggs, beaten
- ½ tsp. ginger, ground
- 2 tsp. low-sodium soy sauce
- 2 tbsp. olive oil
- 1 onion, diced
- 4 garlic cloves, minced
- 1 cup cremini mushrooms, sliced
- 1 (10-oz.) package brown rice, frozen, thawed
- 8 oz. fresh asparagus, about 15 spears, cut into 1-inch pieces
- 1 tsp. sesame oil

DIRECTIONS:

1. Whisk the eggs, ginger, and soy sauce in a small bowl and set aside.
2. Warm olive oil in a skillet or wok over medium heat.
3. Add the onion and garlic and sauté for 2 minutes until tender-crisp.
4. Add the mushrooms and rice; stir-fry for 3 minutes longer.
5. Put asparagus and cook for 2 minutes.6.
6. Pour in the egg mixture. Stir the eggs until cooked through, 2 to 3 minutes, and stir into the rice mixture.
7. Sprinkle the fried rice with the sesame oil and serve.

NUTRITION:

- Calories: 247 kcal
- Fat: 13 g
- Carbohydrates: 25 g
- Protein: 9 g
- Sodium: 149 mg
- Potassium: 367 mg
- Phosphorus: 206 mg

127. Vegetarian Taco Salad

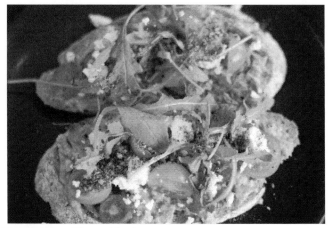

Preparation Time: 15 minutes
Cooking Time: 15 minutes
Servings: 2
INGREDIENTS:

- 1½ cups low-sodium beans, or no-salt-added pinto, canned, rinsed, and drained
- 1 (10-oz.) package brown rice, frozen, thawed
- 1 red bell pepper, chopped
- 3 scallions, white and green parts, chopped
- 1 jalapeño pepper, minced
- 1 cup corn, frozen, thawed, and drained
- 1 tbsp. chili powder
- 1 cup romaine lettuce, chopped
- 2 cups butter lettuce, chopped
- ½ cup Powerhouse Salsa
- ½ cup pepper Jack cheese, grated

DIRECTIONS:

1. Prepare a medium bowl, combine the beans, rice, bell pepper, scallions, jalapeño, and corn.
2. Sprinkle with the chili powder and stir gently.
3. Stir in the romaine and butter lettuce.
4. Serve topped with Powerhouse Salsa and cheese.

NUTRITION:

- Calories: 254 kcal
- Fat: 7 g
- Carbohydrates: 39 g
- Protein: 11 g
- Sodium: 440 mg
- Potassium: 599 mg
- Phosphorus: 240 mg

SALAD RECIPES

128. Grapes Jicama Salad

Preparation Time: 5 minutes
Cooking Time: 1 hour
Servings: 2
INGREDIENTS:

- 1 jicama, peeled and sliced
- 1 carrot, sliced
- ½ medium red onion, sliced
- 1 ¼ cup grapes, seedless
- ⅓ cup fresh basil leaves
- 1 tbsp. apple cider vinegar
- 1 ½ tbsp. lemon juice
- 1 ½ tbsp. lime juice

DIRECTIONS:

1. Prepare all salad ingredients into a suitable salad bowl.
2. Toss them well and refrigerate them for 1 hour.
3. Serve.

NUTRITION:

- Calories: 203 kcal
- Fat: 0.7 g
- Sodium: 44 mg
- Carbohydrate: 48.2 g
- Dietary Fiber: 18.4 g
- Protein: 3.7 g
- Sodium: 630 mg
- Potassium: 429 mg
- Phosphorous: 141 mg

129. Butterscotch Apple Salad

Preparation Time: 8 minutes
Cooking Time: 1 hour
Servings: 6
INGREDIENTS:

- 3 cups jazz apples, chopped
- 8 oz. pineapple, canned, crushed
- 8 oz. whipped topping
- ½ cup butterscotch topping
- ⅓ cup almonds
- ¼ cup butterscotch chips

DIRECTIONS:

1. Place all salad ingredients into a suitable salad bowl.
2. Mix well and refrigerate for 1 hour.
3. Serve.

NUTRITION:

- Calories: 293 kcal
- Fat: 12.7 g
- Sodium: 152 mg
- Phosphorous: 202 mg
- Potassium: 296 mg
- Carbohydrate: 45.5 g
- Dietary Fiber: 4.2 g
- Protein: 4.2 g

130. Cranberry Slaw

Preparation Time: 8 minutes
Cooking Time: 5 minutes
Servings: 4
INGREDIENTS:

- ½ medium cabbage head, shredded
- 1 medium red apple, shredded
- 2 tbsp. onion, sliced
- ½ cup cranberries, dried
- ¼ cup almonds, toasted sliced
- ½ cup olive oil
- ¼ tsp. stevia
- ¼ cup cider vinegar
- ½ tbsp. celery seed
- ½ tsp. dry mustard
- ½ cup cream

DIRECTIONS:

1. Take a suitable salad bowl.
2. Start tossing in all the ingredients.
3. Mix well and serve.

NUTRITION:

- Calories: 308 kcal
- Fat: 24.5 g
- Sodium: 23 mg
- Phosphorous: 257 mg
- Potassium: 219 mg
- Carbohydrate: 13.5 g
- Protein: 2.6 g

131. Balsamic Beet Salad

Preparation Time: 10 minutes
Cooking Time: 0 minutes
Servings: 2
INGREDIENTS:

- 1 cucumber, peeled and sliced
- 15 oz. low-sodium beets, canned, sliced
- 4 tsp. balsamic vinegar
- 2 tsp. sesame oil
- 2 tbsp. Gorgonzola cheese

DIRECTIONS:

1. Take a suitable salad bowl.
2. Mix all the ingredients.
3. Serve.

NUTRITION:

- Calories: 145 kcal
- Fat: 7.8 g
- Sodium: 426 mg
- Phosphorus: 79 mg
- Potassium: 229 mg
- Carbohydrate: 16.4 g
- Protein: 5 g

132. Egg Celery Salad

Preparation Time: 10 minutes
Cooking Time: 1 hour
Servings: 4

INGREDIENTS:

- 4 eggs, boiled, peeled, and chopped
- ¼ cup celery, chopped
- ½ cup sweet onion, chopped
- 2 tbsp. sweet pickle, chopped
- 3 tbsp. mayonnaise
- 1 tbsp. mustard

DIRECTIONS:

1. Boil the 4 eggs and cut them into dice once cool.
2. Put all salad ingredients into a suitable salad bowl.
3. Refrigerate for 1 hour.
4. Serve.

NUTRITION:

- Calories: 134 kcal
- Fat: 8.9 g
- Sodium: 259 mg
- Phosphorous: 357 mg
- Potassium: 113 mg
- Carbohydrate: 7.4 g
- Protein: 6.8 g

133. Chicken Orange Salad

Preparation Time: 10 minutes
Cooking Time: 0 minutes
Servings: 4
INGREDIENTS:

- 1 ½ cup chicken, cooked and sliced in dice
- ½ cup celery, diced
- ½ cup green pepper, chopped
- ¼ cup onion, sliced
- 1 cup orange, peeled, cut into segments
- ¼ cup mayonnaise
- ½ tsp. black pepper

DIRECTIONS:

1. Prepare a suitable salad bowl.
2. Start tossing in all the ingredients.
3. Mix well and serve.

NUTRITION:

- Calories: 167 kcal
- Fat: 6.6 g
- Sodium: 151 mg
- Phosphorous: 211 mg
- Potassium: 249 mg
- Carbohydrate: 11.2 g
- Protein: 16 g

134. Almond Pasta Salad

Preparation Time: 10 minutes
Cooking Time: 10 minutes
Servings: 6
INGREDIENTS:

- 1 lb. elbow macaroni, cooked
- ½ cup tomatoes, sun-dried, diced
- 1 (15 oz.) can make whole artichokes, diced
- 1 orange bell pepper, diced
- 3 green onions, sliced
- 2 tbsp. basil, sliced
- 2 oz. almonds, slivered

Dressing:

- 1 garlic clove, minced
- 1 tbsp. Dijon mustard
- 1 tbsp. raw honey
- ¼ cup white balsamic vinegar
- ⅓ cup olive oil

DIRECTIONS:

1. Prepare the oven to 350°F.
2. Lay the almonds on a baking sheet and bake until golden brown.
3. Cook the pasta as per the package instruction.
4. Move to a serving bowl and start tossing all the ingredients.
5. Mix well and serve.

NUTRITION:

- Calories: 260 kcal
- Fat: 7.7 g
- Sodium: 143 mg
- Phosphorus: 39 mg
- Potassium: 585 mg
- Carbohydrate: 41.4 g
- Protein: 9.6 g

135. Pineapple Berry Salad

Preparation Time: 10 minutes
Cooking Time: 5 minutes
Servings: 4
INGREDIENTS:

- 4 cups pineapple, peeled and cubed
- 3 cups strawberries, chopped
- ¼ cup honey
- ½ cup basil leaves
- 1 tbsp. lemon zest
- ½ cup blueberries

DIRECTIONS:

1. Prepare a salad bowl.
2. Put all the ingredients.
3. Mix well and serve.

NUTRITION:

- Calories: 128 kcal
- Fat: 0.6 g
- Sodium: 3 mg
- Phosphorous: 151 mg
- Potassium: 362 mg
- Carbohydrate: 33.1 g
- Protein: 1.8 g

136. Cabbage Pear Salad

Preparation Time: 15 minutes
Cooking Time: 1 hour
Servings: 6
INGREDIENTS:

- 2 scallions, chopped
- 2 cups green cabbage, finely shredded
- 1 cup red cabbage, finely shredded
- ½ red bell pepper, boiled and chopped
- ½ cup cilantro, chopped
- 2 celery stalks, chopped
- 1 Asian pear, cored and grated
- ¼ cup olive oil
- Juice of 1 lime
- Zest of 1 lime
- 1 tsp. sugar, granulated

DIRECTIONS:

1. Add cabbages, scallions, celery, pear, red pepper, and cilantro in a mixing bowl.
2. Combine to mix well with each other.
3. Take another mixing bowl; add olive oil, lime juice, lime zest, and sugar. Mix well with each other.
4. Add dressing over and toss well.
5. Refrigerate for 1 hour; serve chilled.

NUTRITION:

- Calories: 128 kcal
- Fat: 8 g
- Sodium: 57 mg
- Potassium: 149 mg
- Phosphorus: 25 mg
- Carbohydrates: 2 g
- Protein: 6 g

137. Brie and Apple Salad

Preparation Time: 5 minutes
Cooking Time: 5 minutes
Servings: 2
INGREDIENTS:

- ½ cup, sliced Brie
- ½ apple, peeled, cored and diced
- 1 cup Watercress
- 1 tsp. White vinegar

DIRECTIONS:

1. Toss the watercress in vinegar and scatter with brie and apple.
2. Serve with Melba toast or crackers.

NUTRITION:

- Calories: 111 kcal
- Fat: 7 g
- Carb: 8 g
- Sodium: 7 mg
- Potassium: 99 mg
- Phosphorus: 20 mg
- Protein: 5 g

138. Farfalle Confetti Salad

Preparation Time: 15 minutes
Cooking Time: 10 minutes
Servings: 6
INGREDIENTS:

- 2 cups farfalle pasta, cooked
- ¼ cup red bell pepper, boiled and finely chopped
- ¼ cup cucumber, finely chopped
- ¼ cup carrot, grated
- 2 tbsp. yellow bell pepper
- ½ scallion, green part only, finely chopped
- ½ cup homemade mayonnaise
- 1 tbsp. lemon juice, freshly squeezed
- 1 tsp. fresh parsley, chopped
- ½ tsp. sugar, granulated
- Black pepper, freshly ground

DIRECTIONS:

1. In a bowl, toss together the pasta, red pepper, carrot, cucumber, yellow pepper, and scallion.
2. Prepare a bowl, whisk together the mayonnaise, parsley, lemon juice, and sugar.
3. Put dressing in the pasta mixture and stir to combine.
4. Season with pepper.
5. Chill for 1 hour and serve.

NUTRITION:

- Calories: 119 kcal
- Fat: 3 g
- Carb: 20 g
- Sodium: 16 mg
- Potassium: 82 mg
- Phosphorus: 51 mg
- Protein: 4 g

139.   Tarragon and Pepper Pasta Salad

Preparation Time: 10 minutes
Cooking Time: 35 minutes
Servings: 4
INGREDIENTS:

- 2 cups cooked pasta
- 1 red bell pepper, finely diced
- ½ cucumber, finely diced
- ¼ red onion, finely diced
- 1 tsp. black pepper
- 2 tbsp. extra virgin olive oil
- 1 tbsp. tarragon, dried

DIRECTIONS:

1. Cook pasta according to package directions.
2. Cool and combine the rest of the raw ingredients and mix well.
3. Serve.

NUTRITION:

- Calories: 157 kcal
- Fat: 8 g
- Carb: 24 g
- Sodium: 5 mg
- Potassium: 95 mg
- Phosphorus: 61 mg
- Protein: 11 g

140.   Beet Feta Salad

Preparation Time: 10 minutes
Cooking Time: 30 minutes
Servings: 5
INGREDIENTS:

- 4 cups baby salad greens
- ½ sweet onion, sliced
- 8 small beets, trimmed

- 2 tbsp. + 1 tsp. extra-virgin olive oil
- 1 tbsp. white wine vinegar
- 1 tsp. Dijon mustard
- Black pepper, ground, to taste
- 2 tbsp. feta cheese, crumbled
- 2 tbsp. walnut pieces

DIRECTIONS:

1. Prepare an oven to 400°F. Grease an aluminum foil with some cooking spray.
2. Add beets with 1 tsp. of olive oil; combine and wrap foil.
3. Bake for 30 minutes until it becomes tender. Cut beets into wedges.
4. Add remaining olive oil, vinegar, black pepper, and mustard in a mixing bowl. Combine to mix well with each other.
5. In a mixing bowl, add salad greens, onion, feta cheese, and walnuts. Combine to mix well with each other.
6. Add half of the prepared vinaigrette and toss well.
7. Add beet and combine well.
8. Drizzle the remaining vinaigrette and serve fresh.

NUTRITION:

- Calories: 184 kcal
- Fat: 9 g
- Sodium: 235 mg
- Potassium: 601 mg
- Phosphorus: 98 mg
- Carbohydrates: 19 g
- Protein: 4 g

141.   Creamed Chicken Salad

Preparation Time: 15 minutes
Cooking Time: 20 minutes
Servings: 4
INGREDIENTS:

- 2 chicken breasts, skinless and boneless
- 1 tsp. Dijon mustard
- 2 tsp. lemon juice, freshly squeezed
- 1 cup mayonnaise, preferably homemade

- 4 scallions, trimmed and thinly sliced

DIRECTIONS:

1. Put chicken in a stockpot and bring to a boil.
2. Then, continue to simmer for 13 to 16 minutes (a meat thermometer should read 165°F).
3. Cut the chicken into strips and arrange in a serving bowl. Toss the chicken with the remaining ingredients.
4. Serve with fresh coriander if desired.

NUTRITION:

- Calories: 250 kcal
- Fat: 2.3 g
- Sodium: 213 mg
- Potassium: 475 mg
- Phosphorus: 243 mg
- Carbs: 23 g
- Protein: 25.7 g

142. Chicken Cranberry Sauce Salad

Preparation Time: 10 minutes
Cooking Time: 1 hour
Servings: 6
INGREDIENTS:

- 3 cups chicken meat, cooked, cubed
- 1 cup grapes
- 2 cups carrots, shredded
- ¼ red onion, chopped
- 1 large yellow bell pepper, chopped
- ¼ cup mayonnaise
- ½ cup cranberry sauce

DIRECTIONS:

1. Get all the salad ingredients in a large salad bowl.
2. Toss them well and refrigerate them for 1 hour.
3. Serve.

NUTRITION:

- Calories: 240 kcal
- Fat: 8.6 g
- Sodium: 161 mg
- Phosphorous: 260 mg
- Potassium: 351 mg
- Carbohydrate: 19.4 g
- Protein: 21 g

143. Cucumber-Carrot Salad

Preparation Time: 15 minutes
Cooking Time: 45 minutes
Servings: 2
INGREDIENTS:

- ¼ cup seasoned rice vinegar
- 1 tsp. white sugar
- ½ tsp. vegetable oil
- ¼ tsp. salt
- ¼ tsp. ginger, grated and peeled
- 1 cup carrot, sliced
- 2 tbsp. green onion, sliced
- 2 tbsp. red bell pepper, minced
- ½ cucumber

DIRECTIONS:

1. Cut the cucumber into halved lengthwise and seeded.
2. Put the rice vinegar, sugar, vegetable oil, ginger, and salt together in a bowl.
1. Mix until sugar and salt are dissolved into a smooth dressing.
2. Toss the carrot, green onion, bell pepper, and cucumber in the dressing to coat evenly.
3. Cover the bowl and refrigerate until chilled, about 30 minutes.

NUTRITION:

- Calories: 25 kcal
- Fat: 0 g
- Carbs: 6 g
- Protein: 0 g
- Sodium: 22 mg
- Potassium: 180 mg
- Phosphorus: 22 mg

144. Mediterranean Couscous Salad

Preparation Time: 15 minutes
Cooking Time: 10 minutes
Servings: 5
INGREDIENTS:

- 1 cup couscous, uncooked, or 3 cups cooked
- 1 English cucumber, chopped
- 10 oz. cherry tomatoes, halved
- ½ cup green bell pepper, chopped
- ¼ cup red onion, chopped
- 1 cup olives, halved
- 15 oz. can chickpeas, drained and rinsed
- ½ cup feta cheese
- 2 tbsp. lemon juice
- 1 tbsp. olive oil
- ½ tsp. salt
- ¼ tsp. black pepper
- ½ tsp. oregano, dried
- 1 tbsp. fresh parsley, chopped

DIRECTIONS:

1. Prepare couscous according to package directions
2. Prepare salad bowl, put the sliced cucumber, cherry tomatoes, bell pepper, onion, olives, chickpeas, and cheese. Put the couscous and toss it together.
3. Add some lemon juice and olive oil to the salad. Toss gently.
4. Season with oregano, salt, and pepper.
5. Serve immediately or keep in refrigerator until ready to serve.

NUTRITION:

- Calories: 121 kcal
- Fat: 6 g
- Carbs: 14 g
- Protein: 3 g
- Sodium: 167 mg
- Potassium: 105 mg
- Phosphorus: 51 mg

145. Jicama and Carrot Salad with Honey-Lime Dressing

Preparation Time: 15 minutes
Cooking Time: 15 minutes
Servings: 8
INGREDIENTS:
The Dressing:

- 10 tbsp. +2 tsp. fresh lime juice
- ¾ tsp. honey or agave nectar
- ¼ tsp. cumin, ground
- ⅛ tsp. salt
- 1 tbsp. + 2 tsp. extra-virgin olive oil

The Salad:

- 1 lb. jicama, peeled and thinly sliced
- 2 large carrots grated
- 3 tbsp. cilantro, minced
- ½ jalapeno pepper, seeded and minced

DIRECTIONS:
The Dressing:

1. Get a small bowl, whisk together the lime juice, honey, or agave nectar,
2. cumin, and salt. Slowly whisk in the olive0oil.

The Salad:

1. In a large bowl, toss together the jicama, carrot, cilantro, and jalapeno pepper.
2. Add the dressing and toss to coat. Serve.

NUTRITION:

- Calories: 75 kcal
- Fat: 3 g
- Carbs: 11 g
- Protein: 1 g
- Sodium: 12 mg
- Potassium: 130 mg
- Phosphorus: 15 mg

146.   Easy Caramel Apple Salad

Preparation Time: 10 minutes
Cooking Time: 40 minutes
Servings: 12
INGREDIENTS:

- 1 (8 oz.) whipped topping, frozen and thawed
- 1 (8 oz.) can pineapple, crushed
- 1 (3.4 oz.) instant butterscotch pudding mix
- 2 cups apples, chopped
- 1 cup peanuts, skinless

DIRECTIONS:

1. Stir whipped topping, pineapple, and butterscotch pudding mix together in a bowl until smooth.
2. Fold apples and peanuts into a pudding mixture until salad is well mixed.
3. Refrigerate salad until completely chilled, at least 30 minutes.

NUTRITION:

- Calories: 196 kcal
- Fat: 8 g
- Carbs: 30 g
- Protein: 1 g
- Sodium: 37 mg
- Potassium: 105 mg
- Phosphorus: 47 mg

147.   Pineapple Shrimp Salad

Preparation Time: 10 minutes
Cooking Time: 20 minutes
Servings: 4
INGREDIENTS:

- 2 baby pineapples, or 1 large pineapple
- 1 small English cucumber, diced
- ½ jalapeno, or to taste
- 1 avocado
- Juice of 1 lime
- ¼ tsp. Sriracha
- ¼ cup fresh cilantro, chopped
- 1-lb. shrimp, cooked
- Salt and pepper to taste

DIRECTIONS:

1. Remove the stem and seeds of jalapeno, then finely chop.
2. Peeled, core, and cube the avocado.
3. Slice pineapples down the middle. Cut the perimeter of the inside.
4. Make inner flesh into 4 blocks and then take out.
5. Get ¼ cup of the pineapple flesh and crush, creating a liquid juice—slice remaining pineapple into small cubes.
6. Put shrimp, cucumber, jalapeno, avocado, lime, cilantro, and Sriracha to the pineapple.
7. Flavor with salt and pepper.
8. Scoop the mix back into the hollowed-out pineapples and serve.

NUTRITION:

- Calories: 278 kcal
- Fat: 18 g
- Carbs: 7 g
- Protein: 22 g
- Sodium: 345 mg
- Potassium: 450 mg
- Phosphorus: 255 mg

SEASONAL RECIPES

148. 5 Ingredients Pasta

Preparation Time: 15 minutes
Cooking Time: 25 minutes
Servings: 5
INGREDIENTS:

- 1 (25 oz.) jar marinara sauce
- Olive oil, as needed
- 1-lb. dry vegan pasta
- 1-lb. assorted vegetables, like red onion, zucchini, and tomatoes
- ¼ cup prepared hummus
- Salt, to taste

DIRECTIONS:

1. Prepare oven to 400°F and grease a large baking sheet.
2. Arrange the vegetables in a single layer on the baking sheet and sprinkle them with olive oil and salt.
3. Transfer into the oven and roast the vegetables for about 15 minutes.
4. Boil salted water in a large pot and cook the pasta according to the package directions.
5. Drain the water when the pasta is tender and put the pasta in a colander.
6. Mix the marinara sauce and hummus in a large pot to make a creamy sauce.
7. Stir in the cooked vegetables and pasta to the sauce and toss to coat well.
8. Dish out in a bowl and serve warm.

NUTRITION:

- Calories: 472 kcal
- Fat: 14.5 g
- Carbohydrates: 72.3 g
- Protein: 13.9 g

149. Plant-Based Keto Lo Mein

Preparation Time: 10 minutes
Cooking Time: 10 minutes
Servings: 2
INGREDIENTS:

- 2 tbsp. carrots, shredded
- 1 package kelp noodles, soaked in water
- 1 cup broccoli, frozen

For the Sauce:

- 1 tbsp. sesame oil
- 2 tbsp. tamari

- ½ tsp. ginger, ground
- ¼ tsp. Sriracha
- ½ tsp. garlic powder

DIRECTIONS:

1. Put the broccoli in a saucepan on medium-low heat and add the sauce ingredients.
2. Cook for about 5 minutes and add the noodles after draining water.
3. Allow simmering for about 10 minutes, occasionally stirring to avoid burning.
4. When the noodles have softened, mix everything well and dish out to serve.

NUTRITION:

- Calories: 97 kcal
- Fat: 7 g
- Carbohydrates: 6.2 g
- Protein: 3.4 g

150. Veggie Noodles

Preparation Time: 10 minutes
Cooking Time: 5 minutes
Servings: 2
INGREDIENTS:

- 2 tbsp. vegetable oil
- 4 spring onions, divided
- 1 cup snap pea
- 2 tbsp. brown sugar
- 9 oz. dried rice noodles, cooked
- 5 garlic cloves, minced
- 2 carrots, cut into small sticks
- 3 tbsp. soy sauce

DIRECTIONS:

1. Prepare a skillet, add vegetable oil, and warm over medium heat. Add garlic and 3 spring onions.
2. Cook for about 3 minutes and add the carrots, peas, brown sugar, and soy sauce.
3. Add rice noodles and cook for about 2 minutes.
4. Season with salt and black pepper and top with remaining spring onion to serve.

NUTRITION:

- Calories: 411
- Fat: 14.3g
- Carbohydrates: 63.6g
- Protein: 8.1g

151. Stir Fry Noodles

Preparation Time: 10 minutes
Cooking Time: 8 minutes
Servings: 4
INGREDIENTS:

- 1 cup broccoli, chopped
- 1 cup red bell pepper, chopped
- 1 cup mushrooms, chopped
- 1 large onion, chopped
- 1 batch Stir Fry Sauce, prepared
- Salt and black pepper, to taste
- 2 cups spaghetti, cooked
- 4 garlic cloves, minced
- 2 tbsp. sesame oil

DIRECTIONS:

1. Warm sesame oil in a pan over medium heat and add garlic, onions, bell pepper, broccoli, mushrooms.
2. Sauté for about 5 minutes and add spaghetti noodles and stir fry sauce.
3. Mix well and cook for 3 more minutes.
4. Dish out in plates and serve to enjoy.

NUTRITION:

- Calories: 286 kcal
- Fat: 8.5 g
- Carbohydrates: 44.1 g
- Protein: 9.3 g

152. Spicy Sweet Chili Veggie Noodles

Preparation Time: 10 minutes
Cooking Time: 7 minutes
Servings: 2
INGREDIENTS:

- 1 head broccoli
- 1 onion, finely sliced
- 1 tbsp. olive oil
- 1 Courgette, halved
- 2 nests whole-wheat noodles
- 150 g mushrooms, sliced

For Sauce:

- 3 tbsp. soy sauce
- ¼ cup sweet chili sauce
- 1 tsp. Sriracha
- 1 tbsp. peanut butter
- 2 tbsp. water, boiled

For Topping:

- 2 tsp. sesame seeds

- 2 tsp. chili flakes, dried

DIRECTIONS:

1. Slice the broccoli into bite-sized florets
2. Prepare a pan with warm olive oil on medium flame, then add onions.
3. Sauté for about 2 minutes and add broccoli, Courgette, and mushrooms.
4. Cook and occasionally stir for about 5 minutes.
5. Whisk sweet chili sauce, soy sauce, Sriracha, water, and peanut butter in a bowl.
6. Cook noodles based on the packet directions and add to the vegetables.
7. Stir in the sauce and top with dried chili flakes and sesame seeds to serve.

NUTRITION:

- Calories: 490 kcal
- Fat: 16.4 g
- Carbohydrates: 70.9 g
- Protein: 16.8 g

153. Creamy Vegan Mushroom Pasta

Preparation Time: 10 minutes
Cooking Time: 30 minutes
Servings: 6
INGREDIENTS:

- 2 cups peas, frozen and thawed
- 3 tbsp. flour, unbleached
- 3 cups almond breeze, unsweetened
- 1 tbsp. nutritional yeast
- ⅓ cup fresh parsley
- ¼ cup olive oil
- 1-lb. pasta of choice
- 4 garlic cloves, minced
- ⅔ cup shallots, chopped
- 8 cups mixed mushrooms, sliced
- Salt and black pepper, to taste

DIRECTIONS:

1. Chop the parsley, add more for garnish.
2. Take a bowl and boil pasta in salted water.
3. Get a pan, then add olive oil and heat over medium heat.
4. Add mushrooms, garlic, shallots, and ½ tsp. salt and cook for 15 minutes.
5. Sprinkle flour on the vegetables and stir for a minute while cooking.
6. Add almond beverage, stir constantly.
7. Simmer for 5 minutes before adding pepper to it.
8. Cook for 3 more minutes and remove from heat.
9. Stir in nutritional yeast. Add peas, salt, and pepper.
10. Cook for another minute and add pasta to this sauce.

11. Garnish and serve!

NUTRITION:

- Calories: 321 kcal
- Fat: 5.3 g
- Carbohydrates: 59.4 g
- Protein: 14.3 g

154. Vegan Chinese Noodles

Preparation Time: 15 minutes
Cooking Time: 8 minutes
Servings: 4
INGREDIENTS:

- 300 g mixed oriental mushrooms, such as oyster, shiitake, and enoki, cleaned and sliced
- 200 g thin rice noodles, cooked according to packet directions and drained
- 2 garlic cloves, minced
- 1 fresh red chili
- 200 g Courgette, sliced
- 6 spring onions, reserving the green part
- 1 tsp. corn flour
- 1 tbsp. agave syrup
- 1 tsp. sesame oil
- 100 g baby spinach, chopped
- Hot chili sauce, to serve
- 2(1-inch) pieces of ginger
- ½ bunch fresh coriander, chopped
- 4 tbsp. vegetable oil
- 2 tbsp. low-salt soy sauce
- ½ tbsp. rice wine
- 2 limes to serve

DIRECTIONS:

1. Prepare a pan and heat sesame oil over high heat. Put the mushrooms once heated.
2. Sauté for about 4 minutes and add garlic, chili, ginger, Courgette, coriander stalks, and the white part of the spring onions.
3. Sauté for about 3 minutes until softened and lightly golden.
4. Meanwhile, combine the corn flour and 2 tbsp. of water in a bowl.
5. Add soy sauce, agave syrup, sesame oil, and rice wine to the corn flour mixture.
6. Put this mixture in the pan to the veggie mixture and cook for about 3 minutes until thickened.
7. Add the spinach and noodles and mix well.
8. Stir in the coriander leaves and top with lime wedges, hot chili sauce, and reserved spring onions to serve.

NUTRITION:

- Calories: 269 kcal
- Fat: 15.6 g
- Carbohydrates: 31.8 g
- Protein: 4.8 g

155. Vegetable Penne Pasta

Servings: 6
Preparation Time: 15 minutes
Cooking Time: 20 minutes
INGREDIENTS:

- ½ large onion, chopped
- 2 celery sticks, chopped
- ½ tbsp. ginger paste
- ½ cup green bell pepper
- 1½ tbsp. soy sauce
- ½ tsp. parsley
- Salt and black pepper, to taste
- ½-lb. penne pasta, cooked
- 2 large carrots, diced
- ½ small leek, chopped
- 1 tbsp. olive oil
- ½ tsp. garlic paste
- ½ tbsp. Worcester sauce
- ½ tsp. coriander
- 1 cup water

DIRECTIONS:

1. Prepare a pan on medium heat, then add olive oil. Once heated, add onions, garlic, and ginger paste.
2. Sauté for about 3 minutes and stir in bell pepper, celery sticks, carrots, and leek.
3. Sauté for about 5 minutes and add remaining ingredients except for pasta.
4. Cover the lid and cook for about 12 minutes.
5. Stir in the cooked pasta and dish out to serve warm.

NUTRITION:

- Calories: 167 kcal
- Fat: 3.3 g
- Carbohydrates: 29.5 g
- Protein: 5.2 g

156. Creamy Pumpkin Pasta

Servings: 6
Preparation Time: 15 minutes
Cooking Time: 5 minutes
INGREDIENTS:

- 1 tbsp. olive oil
- 1 cup raw cashews
- 12 oz. penne pasta, dried
- 1 cup pumpkin puree, canned
- 1 cup almond milk
- 3 garlic cloves
- ¼ tsp. nutmeg, ground
- Fresh parsley, for garnish
- 1 tbsp. lemon juice
- ¾ tsp. salt
- 1 tbsp. fresh sage, chopped

DIRECTIONS:

1. Leave cashews in water 4-8 hours, drained, and rinsed
2. Prepare water with salt in a large pot. Once boiling, add the pasta.
3. Cook according to the package directions and drain the pasta into a colander.
4. Dish out the pasta in a large serving bowl and add a dash of olive oil to prevent sticking.
5. Put the pumpkin, cashews, milk, lemon juice, garlic, salt, and nutmeg into the food processor and blend until smooth.
6. Stir in the sauce and sage over the pasta and toss to coat well.
7. Garnish with fresh parsley and dish out to serve hot.

NUTRITION:

- Calories: 425 kcal
- Fat: 24 g
- Carbohydrates: 44.8 g
- Protein: 11.5 g

157. Bake Pasta with Cashew Cream

Preparation Time: 1 hour 10 minutes
Cooking Time: 20 minutes
Servings: 8
INGREDIENTS:
For the Pasta:

- 1 packet penne pasta

For the Bolognese Sauce:

- 1 tbsp. soy sauce
- 1 small can of lentils
- 1 tbsp. brown sugar
- ½ cup tomato paste
- 1 tsp. garlic, crushed
- 1 tbsp. olive oil
- 2 tomatoes, chopped
- 1 onion, chopped
- 2 cups mushrooms, sliced
- Salt, to taste
- Pepper, to taste

For the Cashew Cream:

- 1 cup raw cashews
- ½ lemon, squeezed
- ½ tsp. salt
- ½ cup water

For the White Sauce:

- 1 tsp. black pepper
- 1 tsp. Dijon mustard
- ¼ cup nutritional yeast
- Sea salt, as required
- 2 cups coconut milk
- 3 tbsp. vegan butter
- 2 tbsp. all-purpose flour
- ⅓ cup vegetable broth

DIRECTIONS:

1. Take a pot and boil water, add pasta to it, boil for 3 minutes, and set aside.
2. Fry onion and garlic, mushroom in olive oil, and add soy sauce to it.
3. Add sugar tomato paste, lentils, and canned tomato to it and let it simmer. Bolognese sauce is prepared.
4. Add flavor with salt and black pepper.
5. Add the lemon juice, cashews, water, and salt to the blender, blend for 2 minutes.
6. Add this to the sauce you have prepared and stir pasta in it.
7. Melt the vegan butter in a saucepan, add in the flour, and stir.
8. Add vegetable stock and coconut milk to it and whisk well.
9. Stir continuously and let it boil for about 5 minutes, then remove from heat.
10. Add Dijon mustard, nutritional yeast, black pepper, and sea salt.
11. Preheat the oven to 430°F.

12. Prepare a rectangular oven-safe dish by placing pasta and Bolognese sauce on it.
13. Pour the white sauce on it and bake for 20-25 minutes.

NUTRITION:

- Calories: 395 kcal
- Fat: 28.4 g
- Carbohydrates: 30.8 g
- Protein: 9.3 g

158. Creamy Spinach Pasta

Preparation Time: 8 hours
Cooking Time: 20 minutes
Servings: 4
INGREDIENTS:

- 1 cup raw cashews
- 2 tbsp. lemon juice
- 1 tbsp. olive oil
- 1 ½ cups vegetable broth
- 2 tbsp. fresh dill, chopped
- Red pepper flakes, to taste
- 10 oz. fusilli, dried
- ½ cup unflavored almond milk (unsweetened)
- 2 tbsp. white miso paste
- 4 garlic cloves, divided
- 8-oz. fresh spinach, finely chopped
- ¼ cup scallions, chopped
- Salt and black pepper, to taste

DIRECTIONS:

1. Leave raw cashews in water for 8 hours.
2. Boil salted water in a large pot and add pasta.
3. Cook according to the package directions and drain the pasta into a colander.
4. Dish out the pasta in a large serving bowl and add a dash of olive oil to prevent sticking.
5. Put the cashews, milk, miso, lemon juice, and 1 garlic clove into the food processor and blend until smooth.
6. Put olive oil over medium heat in a large pot and add the remaining 3 cloves.
7. Sauté for about 1 minute and stir in the spinach and broth.
8. Raise the heat and simmer for about 4 minutes until the spinach is bright green and wilted.
9. Stir in the pasta and cashew mixture and season with salt and black pepper.
10. Top with scallions and dill and dish out into plates to serve.

NUTRITION:

- Calories: 603 kcal
- Fat: 28.8 g
- Carbohydrates: 72.3 g
- Protein: 20.2 g

159. Cannellini Pesto Spaghetti

Preparation Time: 5 minutes
Cooking Time: 10 minutes
Servings: 4
INGREDIENTS:

- 12 oz. (340 g) whole-grain spaghetti, cooked, drained, and kept warm
- ½ cup cooking liquid reserved
- 1 cup pesto
- 2 cups cannellini beans, cooked

DIRECTIONS:

1. Rinse and drain the cannellini beans.
2. Put the cooked spaghetti in a large bowl and add the pesto.
3. Add the reserved cooking liquid and beans and toss well to serve.

NUTRITION:

- Calories: 549 kcal
- Fat: 34.9 g
- Carbohydrates: 45.2 g
- Protein: 18.3 g

160. Cold Orange Soba Noodles

Preparation Time: 10 minutes
Cooking Time: 8 minutes
Servings: 4
INGREDIENTS:

- 3 tbsp. mellow white miso
- 1 orange zest and juice of 2 oranges

- 3 tbsp. ginger, grated
- ½ tsp. red pepper flakes, crushed
- 1-lb. (454 g) soba noodles, cooked, drained, and rinsed until cool
- ¼ cup cilantro, chopped
- 4 green onions, chopped

DIRECTIONS:

1. Put the miso, orange zest and juice, ginger, and crushed red pepper flakes in a large bowl and whisk well to combine.
2. Add water as needed. Set the cooked noodles and toss to coat well.
3. Serve garnished with cilantro and green onions.

NUTRITION:

- Calories: 166 kcal
- Fat: 1.1 g
- Carbohydrates: 34.2 g
- Protein: 7.9 g

161. Crispy Tofu and Vegetable Noodles

Preparation Time: 35 minutes
Cooking Time: 30 minutes
Servings: 4
INGREDIENTS:

- 12 oz. (340 g) rice noodles
- 14 oz. (397 g) firm tofu, cut into ¾-inch pieces
- 6 Thai, Serrano chiles, stemmed and deseeded
- 4 shallots, peeled
- 6 garlic cloves, peeled
- 2 cups vegetable broth
- ¼ cup soy sauce
- ¼ cup date sugar (optional)
- 3 tbsp. lime juice (2 limes)
- ⅓ cup cornstarch
- 5 tbsp. vegetable oil, divided (optional)
- 4 (4-oz./113-g) heads baby Bok choy, stalks sliced into ¼-inch-thick, greens sliced into ½ inch thick
- 1 red bell pepper, stemmed, deseeded, sliced into ¼ inch thick, and halved crosswise
- 2 cups fresh Thai basil leaves

Optional:

- Black pepper, ground to taste
- Salt

DIRECTIONS:

1. Cover the noodles with hot water in a large bowl and stir to separate. Let noodles soak until softened, about 35 minutes. Drain noodles.

2. Meanwhile, spread tofu on a paper towel-lined baking sheet and let drain for 20 minutes. Carefully dry with paper towels and season with salt (if desired) and pepper.
3. Meanwhile, pulse chiles, shallots, and garlic in a food processor to smooth paste.
4. Whisk the broth, soy sauce, sugar (if desired), and lime juice together in a medium bowl. Set aside.
5. Toss drained tofu with cornstarch in a separate large bowl, then transfer to a strainer and shake gently to remove excess cornstarch.
6. Heat 2 tbsp. of vegetable oil (if desired) in a skillet over medium-high heat until shimmering.
7. Add tofu and cook, constantly turning, until crisp and well browned on all sides, 14 minutes. Move tofu to a paper towel-lined plate to drain.
8. Heat 1 tbsp. of vegetable oil (if desired) in the skillet over high heat until shimmering.
9. Add the Bok choy stalks and bell pepper and cook until tender and lightly browned, 3 minutes.
10. Stir in Bok choy leaves and cook until lightly wilted, about 30 seconds, transfer to a medium bowl.
11. Heat the remaining vegetable oil (if desired) in the skillet over medium-high heat until shimmering.
12. Add the processed Chile mixture and cook until moisture evaporates, and the color deepens, 4 minutes.
13. Add the noodles and broth mixture to the skillet. Cook until slightly thickened and noodles are well coated and tender for about 5 minutes.
14. Stir in the browned vegetables and basil and cook until warmed through, about 1 minute.
15. Top with crispy tofu and serve.

NUTRITION:

- Calories: 375 kcal
- Fat: 18.3 g
- Carbohydrates: 42. 0g
- Protein: 15.4 g

162. Indonesia Green Noodle Salad

Preparation Time: 10 minutes
Cooking Time: 8 minutes
Servings: 4
INGREDIENTS:

- 12 oz. (340 g) cauliflower rice noodles, cooked, drained, and rinsed until cool
- 1 cup snow peas, trimmed and sliced in half on the diagonal
- 2 medium cucumbers, peeled, halved, deseeded, and sliced thinly
- 2 heads baby Bok choy, trimmed and thinly sliced
- 4 green onions, green and white parts, trimmed and thinly sliced
- 3 tbsp. sambal oelek
- ½ cup cilantro, chopped
- 2 tbsp. soy sauce
- ¼ cup fresh lime juice
- ¼ cup mint, finely chopped

DIRECTIONS:

1. Prepare all ingredients in a large bowl and toss to coat well.
2. Serve immediately.

NUTRITION:

- Calories: 288 kcal
- Fat: 1.1 g
- Carbohydrates: 64.6 g
- Protein: 12.1 g

163. Kimchi Green Rice Noodle Salad

Preparation Time: 10 minutes
Cooking Time: 8 minutes
Servings: 4

INGREDIENTS:

- 1 lb. (454 g) cauliflower rice noodles, cooked, drained, and rinsed until cool
- 2 ½ cups kimchi, chopped
- 3 to 4 tbsp. gochujang
- 1 cup mung bean sprouts
- 1 medium cucumber, halved, deseeded, and thinly sliced
- 4 green onions, thinly sliced
- 2 tbsp. sesame seeds, toasted

DIRECTIONS:

1. Combine the rice noodles, kimchi, gochujang, and mung bean sprouts in a large bowl and toss to mix well.
2. Divide the mixture among 4 serving plates and garnish with cucumber slices, green onions, and sesame seeds. Serve immediately.

NUTRITION:

- Calories: 186 kcal
- Fat: 2.7 g
- Carbohydrates: 35.6 g
- Protein: 6.1 g

164. Lemony Broccoli Penne

Preparation Time: 25 minutes
Cooking Time: 15 minutes
Servings: 4
INGREDIENTS:

- 1 medium yellow onion, thinly sliced and peeled
- 1-lb. (454 g) broccoli rabe, trimmed and cut into 1-inch pieces
- ¼ cup golden raisins
- Zest and juice of 2 lemons
- 4 garlic cloves, peeled and minced
- ½ tsp. red pepper flakes, crushed
- 1-lb. (454 g) whole-grain penne, cooked, drained, and kept warm, ¼ cup cooking liquid reserved
- ¼ cup pine nuts, toasted
- ½ cup basil, chopped

Optional:

- Salt
- black pepper, ground, to taste

DIRECTIONS:

1. Add the onion in a large skillet over medium-high heat and sauté for 10 minutes, or until the onion is lightly browned.
2. Add the broccoli rabe and cook, frequently stirring, until the rabe is tender, about 5 minutes.

3. Add the raisins, lemon zest and juice, garlic, crushed red pepper flakes, cooked pasta, and reserved cooking water.
4. Remove from the heat. Mix well and season with salt (if desired) and pepper. Serve garnished with pine nuts and basil.

NUTRITION:

- Calories: 278 kcal
- Fat: 7.4 g
- Carbohydrates: 49.6 g
- Protein: 8.8 g

165. Ponzu Pea Rice Noodle Salad

Preparation Time: 5 minutes
Cooking Time: 10 minutes
Servings: 4
INGREDIENTS:

- 16 cups water
- 1 lb. (454 g) cauliflower rice noodles
- ½-lb. (227 g) snow peas,
- 3 medium carrots, peeled, cut into matchsticks
- ½ cup Ponzu sauce, unsweetened
- 3 green onions, cut into ¾-inch pieces
- ½ cup cilantro, coarsely chopped

DIRECTIONS:

1. Trim and cut snow peas into matchsticks.
2. Boil water in a pot, put rice noodles, and cook for 10 minutes or until al dente.
3. Add the snow peas and carrots during the last minute of cooking.
4. Drain and rinse the mixture until cooled and place them in a large bowl.
5. Add the ponzu sauce, green onions, and cilantro. Toss well before serving.

NUTRITION:

- Calories: 179 kcal
- Fat: 0.5 g
- Carbohydrates: 39.0 g
- Protein: 4.8 g

166. Shiitake and Bean Sprout Ramen

Preparation Time: 25 minutes
Cooking Time: 1 hour 15 minutes
Servings: 4 to 6
INGREDIENTS:

- 4 oz. (113 g) bean sprouts
- 3 tbsp. soy sauce, divided
- 4 tsp. sesame oil, toasted and divided (optional)
- 1 tbsp. rice vinegar
- 1 onion, chopped
- 1-piece ginger (3-inch), peeled and sliced into ¼-inch thick
- 5 garlic cloves, smashed
- 8 oz. (227 g) shiitake mushrooms, stems removed and reserved, caps sliced thin
- ½-oz. (14 g) kombu
- ¼ cup mirin
- 4 cups vegetable broth
- 20 cups water, divided
- 2 tbsp. red miso
- Salt, to taste (optional)
- 12 oz. (340 g) ramen noodles, dried
- 2 scallions, sliced thinly
- 1 tbsp. black sesame seeds, toasted

DIRECTIONS:

1. Combine the bean sprouts, 1 tsp. soy sauce, 1 tsp. sesame oil (if desired), and vinegar in a small bowl; set aside.
2. Heat the remaining 1 tbsp. sesame oil (if desired) in a large saucepan over medium-high heat until shimmering.
3. Mix in the onion and cook until softened and lightly browned, about 6 minutes. Add ginger and garlic and cook until lightly browned about 2 minutes.
4. Stir in mushroom stems, kombu, mirin, broth, 4 cups of water, and remaining soy sauce and bring to boil.
5. Simmer and lower the heat for 1 hour with cover on.
6. Filter broth through a fine-mesh strainer into a large bowl. Wipe the saucepan clean and return the strained broth to the saucepan.
7. Whisk miso into the broth and bring to a gentle simmer over medium heat, whisking to dissolve miso completely.
8. Stir in mushroom caps and cook until warmed through, about 1 minute, season with salt if desired. Get from the heat and cover to keep warm.
9. Meanwhile, bring 16 cups of water to a boil in a large pot. Add the ramen noodles and 1 tbsp. salt (if desired) and cook, often stirring, until al dente, about 2 minutes.
10. Drain the noodles and divide evenly among serving bowls. Ladle soup over noodles, garnish with bean sprouts, scallions, and sesame seeds. Serve hot.

NUTRITION:

- Calories: 237 kcal
- Fat: 5.6 g
- Carbohydrates: 37.8 g
- Protein: 8.4 g

167. Cabbage Rotelle Provençale

Preparation Time: 8 minutes
Cooking Time: 12 minutes
Servings: 6
INGREDIENTS:

- 2 (15-oz./425-g) cans tomatoes, unsweetened, stewed
- 1 (19-oz./539-g) can white beans, drained and rinsed
- 20 cups water
- 1 (10-oz./283-g) package cabbage Rotelle
- ¼ cup fresh parsley, chopped

DIRECTIONS:

1. Put the beans and tomatoes in a saucepan and heat over medium heat until the mixture thickened and has a sauce consistency.
2. Boil water on a large pot. Add the cabbage Rotelle and cook, uncovered, for 12 minutes.
3. Drain the Rotelle and transfer it into a large bowl. Add the tomato-bean sauce and toss to coat.
4. Sprinkle with fresh parsley before serving.

NUTRITION:

- Calories: 40 kcal
- Fat: 0.7 g
- Carbohydrates: 8.2 g
- Protein: 2.1 g
- Fiber: 4.2 g

168. Shiitake Udon Noodles

Preparation Time: 20 minutes
Cooking Time: 25 minutes
Servings: 4 to 6
INGREDIENTS:

- 1 tbsp. vegetable oil (optional)
- 8 oz. (227 g) shiitake mushrooms, stemmed and sliced thinly
- ½ oz. (14 g) shiitake mushrooms, dried, rinsed, and minced
- ¼ cup mirin
- 3 tbsp. rice vinegar
- 3 tbsp. soy sauce
- 2 garlic cloves, smashed and peeled
- 1 (1-inch) piece ginger, peeled, halved, and smashed
- 1 tsp. sesame oil, toasted (optional)
- 18 cups water, divided
- 1 tsp. Asian chili-garlic sauce, unsweetened
- 1-lb. (454 g) mustard greens, stemmed and chopped into 2-inch pieces
- 1 lb. (454 g) fresh Udon noodles

Optional:

- Black pepper, ground, to taste
- Salt

DIRECTIONS:

1. Heat the vegetable oil (if desired) in a Dutch oven over medium-high heat until shimmering.
2. Put the mushrooms and cook, occasionally stirring until softened and lightly browned, about 5 minutes.
3. Stir in the dried mushrooms, mirin, vinegar, soy sauce, garlic, ginger, sesame oil (if desired), 2 cups of water, and chili-garlic sauce, and bring to a simmer.
4. Reduce the heat to medium-low and simmer until liquid has reduced by half, 8 minutes. Turn off the heat, discard the garlic and ginger, cover the pot to keep warm.
5. Meanwhile, bring 16 cups of water to a boil in a large pot. Add mustard greens and 1 tbsp. salt (if desired) and cook until greens are tender about 5 minutes.
6. Add noodles and cook until greens and noodles are tender about 2 minutes.
7. Reserve ⅓ cup cooking water, drain noodles and greens, and return them to pot.
8. Add sauce and reserved cooking water and toss to combine.
9. Cook over medium-low heat, constantly tossing, until sauce clings to noodles, about 1 minute.
10. Season with salt (if desired) and pepper and serve.

NUTRITION:

- Calories: 184 kcal
- Fat: 3.6 g
- Carbohydrates: 32.6 g
- Protein: 6.7 g

DESSERTS AND SNACKS RECIPES

169. Lemon Meringue Pie

Preparation Time: 15 minutes
Cooking Time: 1 hour
Servings: 1
INGREDIENTS:
For Pie Filling:

- 6 raw egg yolks
- ½ cup lemon juice
- 2 tbsp. lemon zest
- 1 ¼ tbsp. butter, unsalted
- ⅓ cup cornstarch
- 1 ½ cups water
- 1 ⅓ cup sugar or sugar replacement
- ¼ tsp. salt
- 1 pie shell, store-bought

For Meringue:

- 6 egg whites
- 2 ½ tbsp. sugar or sugar replacement
- 1 pinch cream of tartar

DIRECTIONS:
For Pie Filling:

1. Preheat oven to 375°F.
2. Combine cornstarch, water, salt, and sugar in a medium saucepan.
3. Combine by whisking and then turn the stove plate onto medium heat. When the mixture comes to a boil, stir frequently and allow it to boil for 2 minutes.
4. Put the egg yolks into a medium bowl and gradually add the hot mixture to the egg yolks and stir until combined and the mixture is smooth.
5. Put the mixture in the same saucepan and over low heat, cook for 2 more minutes, stirring continuously.

6. Get from heat and stir in lemon zest, lemon juice, and butter. Continue stirring until all the ingredients are completely incorporated into a smooth mixture. Add mixture into the pie shell and set aside.

For Meringue:

1. Beat egg whites and cream of tartar, then gradually add sugar and continue beating until stiff peaks form.
2. Top your still-warm filling with the meringue mixture and bake the pie for 12 minutes or until the meringue is golden.
3. Allow cooling completely before serving

NUTRITION:

- Calories: 28 kcal
- Carbohydrates: 44 g
- Protein: 6 g
- Sodium: 225 mg
- Phosphorus: 66 mg
- Potassium: 153 mg

170. Fresh Fruit Dessert Cups

Preparation Time: 15 minutes
Cooking Time: 30 minutes
Servings: 1
INGREDIENTS:

- 4 sheets (14-inch x 18-inch) phyllo pastry dough
- Non-stick butter-flavored cooking spray
- 1 cup fresh strawberries
- 1 cup fresh raspberries
- 1 cup fresh blueberries
- 3 cups heavy whipped cream

DIRECTIONS:

1. Ready the oven to 400°F. Prepare a 12-cup muffin pan by spraying with butter-flavored non-stick cooking spray.
2. Pack the four sheets of phyllo dough on top of each other, lightly spraying with cooking spray between each layer. Cut dough into four 3 ½-inch squares.
3. Separate squares and place them into a muffin pan to form dessert cups and bake cups for 12 minutes or lightly browned. Allow cooling.
4. Fill each cup with equal amounts of berries and top with a small dollop of heavy whipped cream. Serve immediately.

NUTRITION:

- Calories: 111 kcal
- Carbohydrates: 18 g
- Protein: 2 g
- Sodium: 51 mg
- Phosphorus: 14 mg
- Potassium: 83 mg

171. Caramel-Centered Cookies

Preparation Time: 15 minutes
Cooking Time: 40 minutes
Servings: 1

INGREDIENTS:

- 1 ¾ cups all-purpose flour
- ½ cup margarine, unsalted
- ½ tsp. baking powder
- ½ tsp. baking soda
- 1 ½ cups butterscotch chips
- ½ bag caramel cubes
- 1 cup light brown sugar or sugar replacement
- 3 tbsp. sugar, granulated, or sugar replacement
- 1 large egg
- 2 tsp. vanilla extract

DIRECTIONS:

1. Prepare oven to 350°F. Cream the butter with light brown sugar and granulated sugar using a mixer on a medium setting, until fluffy.
2. Whisk egg and vanilla extract for another 30 seconds.
3. Sift together dry ingredients in a mixing bowl and beat into the butter mixture at a low speed for about 15 seconds. Stir in butterscotch chips.
4. Using a scoop-shaped 1 tbsp. measure, drop dough onto a greased or lined cookie sheet about 3 inches apart.
5. Place one caramel square in the center of each scoop of dough and top with another tbsp. of dough. Roll in your hand until they are round.
6. Bake for 20 minutes or until browned on the edges.

NUTRITION:

- Calories: 210 kcal
- Carbohydrates: 31 g
- Protein: 1.5 g
- Sodium: 67 mg
- Phosphorus: 35 mg
- Potassium: 82 mg

172. Low-Sodium Lb. Cake

Preparation Time: 10 minutes
Cooking Time: 30 minutes
Servings: 1

INGREDIENTS:

- 1 ¼ cup bread flour
- ¼-lb. butter, unsalted
- ¾ cup sugar or sugar replacement
- 2 large eggs, beaten
- 3 oz. non-fat milk or milk alternative

DIRECTIONS:

1. Preheat oven to 375°F. Prepare a pan by lining an 18-inch x 13-inch pan with baking paper.
2. Cream butter gradually adds sugar and beat until fluffy.
3. Add eggs, milk, and flour and mix well.
4. Pour mixture into the lined pan and bake at 375°F for approximately 30 minutes.

NUTRITION:

- Calories: 243 kcal
- Carbohydrates: 31 g
- Protein: 3.7 g
- Sodium: 18 mg
- Phosphorus: 45 mg
- Potassium: 47 mg

173. Dessert Pizza

Preparation Time: 10 minutes
Cooking Time: 15 minutes
Servings: 1
INGREDIENTS:

- 1 (12-inch) pre-cooked pizza base
- 2 cups fresh strawberries, sliced
- 1 cup part-skim ricotta cheese
- ½ cup apricot jam or other light-colored jam
- 5 tbsp. sugar, powdered, or sugar replacement
- 2 tbsp. warm jelly or preserves
- ¼ cup chocolate chips

DIRECTIONS:

1. Preheat oven to 425°F.
2. Strain ricotta. Melt jam in microwave and brush jam on the pizza base.
3. Mix ricotta with 3 tbsp. of powdered sugar and spread it on the pizza base.
4. Arrange strawberry slices on the ricotta layer and sprinkle with remaining powdered sugar and chocolate chips.
5. Bake for 12 minutes, slice, and serve.

NUTRITION:

- Calories: 288 kcal
- Carbohydrates: 49 g
- Protein: 8 g
- Sodium: 166 mg
- Phosphorus: 47 mg
- Potassium: 98 mg

174. Lemon Bars

Preparation Time: 20 minutes
Cooking Time: 45 minutes
Servings: 24

INGREDIENTS:
For Crust:

- 2 cups all-purpose flour
- 1 cup butter, unsalted
- ½ cup sugar, powdered, or sugar replacement

For Filling:

- ¼ cup all-purpose flour
- ¼ tsp. baking soda
- ½ tsp. cream of tartar
- 4 eggs
- 1 ½ cups sugar (alternative: sugar replacement)
- ¼ cup lemon juice

For Glaze:

- 2 tbsp. lemon juice
- 1 cup sifted powdered sugar or sugar replacement

DIRECTIONS:
For Crust:

1. Preheat oven to 350° F. Mix flour, powdered sugar, and butter in a large bowl until crumbly.
2. Press mixture into a 9-inch x 13-inch baking pan.
3. Bake for about 20 minutes until lightly browned.

For Filling:

1. Gently whisk eggs in a medium-sized bowl.
2. Mix flour, sugar, soda, and cream of tartar in a separate bowl and add these ingredients to the eggs. Whisk lemon juice into the egg mixture until slightly thickened.
3. Pour over the warm crust and bake for another 20 minutes or until filling is set. Take away from the oven and allow it to cool.

For Glaze:

1. Slowly add the lemon juice into the sifted powdered sugar until spreadable.
2. Spread over cooled filling. Allow to set and then cut into 24 bars—store leftovers in the refrigerator.

NUTRITION:

- Calories: 200 kcal
- Protein: 2 g
- Carbohydrates: 28 g
- Sodium: 27 mg
- Phosphorus: 32 mg
- Potassium: 41 mg

175. Baked Pineapple

Preparation Time: 10 minutes
Cooking Time: 40 minutes
Servings: 1
INGREDIENTS:

- 20 oz. pineapple with juice, canned, crushed
- 2 large eggs or egg substitute
- 2 cups sugar or sugar replacement
- 3 tbsp. tapioca
- ½ tsp. cinnamon
- ⅛ tsp. salt
- 3 tbsp. butter, unsalted

DIRECTIONS:

1. Preheat oven to 350°F.
2. Put the crushed pineapple with juice into a bowl.
3. Beat 2 eggs and add to crushed pineapple.
4. Put sugar, tapioca, and salt into the pineapple egg mixture.
5. Pour mixture into an 8-inch square baking dish.
6. Cut butter and place on top of pineapple mixture and sprinkle with cinnamon—Bake for 30 minutes.

NUTRITION:

- Calories: 270 kcal
- Carbohydrates: 54 g
- Protein: 2 g
- Sodium: 50 mg
- Phosphorus: 26 mg
- Potassium: 85 mg

176. Kidney-Friendly Vanilla Ice Cream

Preparation Time: 15 minutes
Cooking Time: 1 hour
Servings: 1
INGREDIENTS:

- 1 cup low-cholesterol egg product
- ½ cup sugar
- 2 cups liquid non-dairy creamer
- 1 tbsp. vanilla extract
- Rock salt
- Ice

DIRECTIONS:

1. Beat egg and sugar in a large microwaveable bowl.
2. Stir in non-dairy creamer and microwave for 1 minute, or until mixture thickens. When cool, stir in vanilla.
3. Add the mixture into the center container of the ice cream machine and layer ice and rock salt around a container, alternating layers until the bucket is full.

4. Process according to the manufacturer's instructions for your particular ice cream machine.

NUTRITION:

- Calories: 159 kcal
- Carbohydrates: 22 g
- Protein: 3 g
- Sodium: 64 mg
- Phosphorus: 36 mg
- Potassium: 87 mg

177. Quick Cupcakes

Preparation Time: 10 minutes
Cooking Time: 10 minutes
Servings: 12
INGREDIENTS:

- 1 box angel food cake mix
- 1 box lemon cake mix
- 2 tsp. water
- Non-stick cooking spray

DIRECTIONS:

1. In a large zip-lock bag, pour in angel food cake mix and lemon cake mix. Close plastic bag and shake to mix.
2. Spray a small custard dish with non-stick cooking spray and add three tbsp. of dry cake mix to the dish. Add 2 tbsp. of water and mix with a fork.
3. Microwave on high for 1 minute. Slip the muffin out of the dish and allow it to cool.
4. Repeat this process for as many cupcakes as you require.

NUTRITION:

- Calories: 97 kcal
- Carbohydrates: 21 g
- Protein: 1 g
- Sodium: 163 mg
- Potassium: 17 mg
- Phosphorus: 80 mg

178. Peppermint Crunch Cookies

Preparation Time: 10 minutes
Cooking Time: 30 minutes
Servings: 18
INGREDIENTS:

- 18 peppermint candies
- ¼ tsp. peppermint extract
- 1 ½ cups all-purpose flour
- 1 tsp. baking powder
- ¼ tsp. salt
- ¾ cup sugar or sugar replacement

- ½ cup soft butter, unsalted
- 1 large egg or egg substitute

DIRECTIONS:

1. Put the 12 peppermint candies in a zip-lock bag and lb. with a heavy pan until finely crushed.
2. Add sugar, butter, egg, and peppermint extract to a bowl. Beat ingredients at medium speed until creamy.
3. Mix flour, baking powder, and salt. Add flour mixture and beat until well-combined.
4. Stir in crushed peppermint candy by hand. Refrigerate for one hour.
5. Prepare the oven to 350°F. Crush the remaining peppermint candies in the same method as the first time. Line baking sheets.
6. Shape chilled dough into ¾-inch balls and place on baking sheets about 2 inches apart. Using thumb, make an indentation in each cookie, and top with about ½ tsp. of crushed candy.
7. Bake until edges are lightly browned. Cool cookies completely and store them in a container between pieces of parchment or wax paper.

NUTRITION:

- Calories: 150 kcal
- Carbohydrates: 22 g
- Protein: 2 g
- Sodium: 67 mg
- Potassium: 17 mg
- Phosphorus: 24 mg

179. Sesame Crackers

Preparation Time: 15 minutes
Cooking Time: 12 minutes
Servings: 1
INGREDIENTS:

- 1 cup sesame seeds
- 2 tbsp. grapeseed oil
- 2 large eggs, beaten
- 1 ½ tsp. sea salt
- 3 cups almond flour

DIRECTIONS:

1. Mix the sesame seeds, almond flour, oil, eggs, and salt in a bowl.
2. Divide the dough into 2 portions.
3. Place each into 2 baking sheets lined with parchment paper and cover with parchment paper.
4. Spread the dough between the papers to cover the baking sheet and remove the top paper.
5. Cut the dough into 2-inch squares and bake at 350°F until golden brown for about 12 minutes.

6. Cool before serving.

NUTRITION:

- Calories: 178 kcal
- Fat: 15.6 g
- Carbs: 6 g
- Protein: 6.1 g
- Sodium: 184 mg
- Potassium: 468 mg
- Phosphorus: 0 mg

180. Veggie Snack

Preparation Time: 5 minutes
Cooking Time: 10 minutes
Servings: 1
INGREDIENTS:

- 1 large yellow pepper
- 5 carrots
- 5 stalks celery

DIRECTIONS:

1. Clean the carrots and rinse them under running water.
2. Rinse celery and yellow pepper. Remove seeds of pepper and chop the veggies into small sticks.
3. Put in a bowl and serve.

NUTRITION:

- Calories: 189 kcal
- Fat: 0.5 g
- Carbs: 44.3 g
- Protein: 5 g
- Sodium: 282 mg
- Potassium: 0mg
- Phosphorus: 0mg

181. Healthy Spiced Nuts

Preparation Time: 10 minutes
Cooking Time: 10 minutes
Servings: 4
INGREDIENTS:

- 1 tbsp. extra virgin olive oil
- ¼ cup walnuts
- ¼ cup pecans
- ¼ cup almonds
- ½ tsp. sea salt
- ½ tsp. cumin
- ½ tsp. pepper
- 1 tsp. chili powder

DIRECTIONS:

1. Put the skillet on medium heat and toast the nuts until lightly browned.
2. Prepare the spice mixture and add black pepper, cumin, chili, and salt.
3. Put extra virgin olive oil and sprinkle with spice mixture to the toasted nuts before serving.

NUTRITION:

- Calories: 88 kcal
- Fat: 8 g
- Carbs: 4 g
- Protein: 2.5 g
- Sodium: 51 mg
- Potassium: 88 mg

182. Vinegar and Salt Kale Chips

Preparation Time: 10 minutes
Cooking Time: 12 minutes
Servings: 2
INGREDIENTS:

- 1 head kale, chopped
- 1 tsp. extra virgin olive oil
- 1 tbsp. apple cider vinegar
- ½ tsp. sea salt

DIRECTIONS:

3. Prepare kale in a bowl and put vinegar and extra virgin olive oil.
4. Sprinkle with salt and massage the ingredients with your hands.
5. Spread the kale onto 2 paper-lined baking sheets and bake at 375°F for about 12 minutes or until crispy.
6. Leave for about 10 minutes before serving.

NUTRITION:

- Calories: 152 kcal
- Fat: 8.2 g
- Carbs: 15.2 g
- Protein: 4 g
- Sodium: 170mg
- Potassium: 304mg
- Phosphorus: 37mg

183. Carrot and Parsnips French Fries

Preparation Time: 15 minutes
Cooking Time: 20 minutes
Servings: 2
INGREDIENTS:

- 6 large carrots
- 6 large parsnips
- 2 tbsp. extra virgin olive oil
- ½ tsp. sea salt

DIRECTIONS:

1. Chop the carrots and parsnips into 2-inch slices and then cut each into thin sticks.
2. Toss together the carrots and parsnip stick with extra virgin olive oil and salt in a bowl and spread into a baking sheet lined with parchment paper.
3. Bake the sticks at 425°F for about 20 minutes or until browned.

NUTRITION:

- Calories: 179 kcal
- Fat: 4 g
- Carbs: 14 g
- Protein: 11 g
- Sodium: 27.3 mg
- Potassium: 625 mg
- Phosphorus: 116 mg

184. Apple and Strawberry Snack

Preparation Time: 5 minutes
Cooking Time: 2 minutes
Servings: 1
INGREDIENTS:

- ½ apple, cored and sliced
- 2-3 strawberries
- A dash cinnamon, ground
- 2-3 drops stevia

DIRECTIONS:

1. In a bowl, mix strawberries and apples and sprinkle with stevia and cinnamon.

2. Microwave for about 1-2 minutes. Serve warm.

NUTRITION:

- Calories: 145 kcal
- Fat: 0.8 g
- Carbs: 34.2 g
- Protein: 1.6 g
- Sodium: 20 mg
- Potassium: 0 mg
- Phosphorus: 0 mg

185. Candied Macadamia Nuts

Preparation Time: 5 minutes
Cooking Time: 15 minutes
Servings: 2
INGREDIENTS:

- 2 cups macadamia nuts
- 1 tbsp. extra-virgin olive oil
- 2 tbsp. honey

DIRECTIONS:

1. Toss ingredients in a bowl and spread into a baking dish.
2. Bake for 15 minutes at 350°F.
3. Let cool before serving.

NUTRITION:

- Calories: 200 kcal
- Fat: 18 g
- Carbs: 10 g
- Protein: 1 g
- Sodium: 5 mg
- Potassium: 55 mg
- Phosphorus: 10mg

186. Cinnamon Apple Chips

Preparation Time: 5 minutes
Cooking Time: 15 minutes
Servings: 1
INGREDIENTS:

- 1 apple, thinly sliced
- Dash cinnamon
- Stevia

DIRECTIONS:

1. Coat apple slices with cinnamon and stevia.
2. Bake for 15 minutes or until tender and crispy at 325°F.

NUTRITION:

- Calories: 146 kcal
- Fat: 0.7 g
- Carbs: 36.4 g

- Protein: 1.6 g
- Sodium: 10 mg
- Potassium: 100mg
- Phosphorus: 0mg

187. Lemon Pops

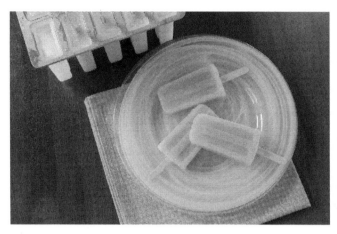

Preparation Time: 5 minutes
Cooking Time: 5 minutes
Servings: 1
INGREDIENTS:

- 4 tbsp. fresh lemon juice
- Powdered stevia

DIRECTIONS:

1. Mix orange or lemon juice and stevia and pour into molds.
2. Freeze until firm.

NUTRITION:

- Calories: 46 kcal
- Fat: 0.2 g
- Carbs: 16 g
- Protein: 0.9 g
- Sodium: 3.7 mg
- Potassium: 104 mg
- Phosphorus: 11 mg

188. Easy No-Bake Coconut Cookies

Preparation Time: 5 minutes
Cooking Time: 10 minutes
Servings: 20
INGREDIENTS:

- 3 cups coconut flakes, finely shredded
- 1 cup coconut oil, melted
- 1 tsp. liquid stevia

DIRECTIONS:

1. Prepare all ingredients in a large bowl; stir until well blended.
2. Form the mixture into small balls and arrange them on a paper-lined baking tray.
3. Press each cookie down with a fork and refrigerate until firm. Enjoy!

NUTRITION:

- Calories: 99 kcal
- Fat: 10 g
- Carbs: 2 g
- Protein: 3 g
- Sodium: 7 mg
- Potassium: 105mg
- Phosphorus: 11mg

189. Roasted Chili-Vinegar Peanuts

Preparation Time: 5 minutes
Cooking Time: 10 minutes
Servings: 4
INGREDIENTS:

- 1 tbsp. coconut oil
- 2 cups raw peanuts, unsalted
- 2 tsp. sea salt
- 2 tbsp. apple cider vinegar
- 1 tsp. chili powder
- 1 tsp. fresh lime zest

DIRECTIONS:

1. Preheat oven to 350°F.
2. Toss together coconut oil, peanuts, and salt in a large bowl until well coated.
3. Move to a rimmed baking sheet and roast in the oven for about 15 minutes or until fragrant.
4. Transfer the roasted peanuts to a bowl and add vinegar, chili powder, and lime zest.
5. Toss to coat well and serve.

NUTRITION:

- Calories: 447 kcal
- Fat: 39.5 g
- Carbs: 12.3 g
- Protein: 18.9 g
- Sodium: 160 mg
- Potassium: 200mg
- Phosphorus: 0mg

JUICE AND SMOOTHIE

190. Holiday Cider

Preparation Time: 10 minutes
Cooking Time: 2 hours
Servings: 8
INGREDIENTS:

- 1 orange
- 2 tsp. whole clove
- 1 apple
- 1 tsp. whole allspice
- 4 cinnamon sticks
- 1 gal apple cider (4 L)
- ½ cup brown sugar (110 g)
- 1 tsp. nutmeg
- Whiskey, or rum, optional

DIRECTIONS:

1. Season orange with cloves. (If you have an infuser, tea bag, or cheesecloth, you can use that to keep the spices under control).
2. Pierce apple with allspice.
3. Put the orange, apple, cinnamon sticks, apple cider, brown sugar, and nutmeg into your slow cooker.
4. Set on high for 2 hours, then keep warm on low until you're ready to drink.
5. Drink as is or with a shot (or two) of whiskey, rum, etc. Enjoy.

NUTRITION:

- Calories: 98 kcal
- Fat: 0.3 g
- Carbs: 27 g
- Protein: 1 g
- Sodium: 2.6 mg
- Potassium: 84.6 mg
- Phosphorus: 16 mg

191. Carrot Peach Water

Preparation Time: 5 minutes
Cooking Time: 10 minutes
Servings: 10
INGREDIENTS:

- 2 peaches, peeled, pitted, and chopped
- 1 large carrot, peeled and grated
- 1-inch piece peeled fresh ginger, lightly crushed
- 3 fresh thyme sprigs
- 10 cups water

DIRECTIONS:

1. Place the peaches, carrot, ginger, and thyme in a large pitcher.
2. Pour in the water and stir the mixture.
3. Place the pitcher in the refrigerator and leave to infuse overnight if possible.
4. Serve cold.

NUTRITION:

- Calories: 140 kcal
- Fat: 0 g
- Carbs: 36 g
- Protein: 0 g
- Sodium: 30 mg
- Potassium: 0 mg
- Phosphorus: 0 mg

192. Papaya Mint Water

Preparation Time: 5 minutes
Cooking Time: 5 minutes
Servings: 10
INGREDIENTS:

- 1 cup fresh papaya, peeled, seeded, and diced
- 2 tbsp. fresh mint leaves, chopped
- 10 cups water, distilled or filtered

DIRECTIONS:

1. Place the papaya and mint in a large pitcher. Pour in the water.
2. Stir and place the pitcher in the refrigerator to infuse overnight if possible.
3. Serve cold.

NUTRITION:

- Calories: 5 kcal
- Fat: 1 g
- Carbs: 1 g
- Protein: 2 g
- Sodium: 15 mg
- Potassium: 0 mg
- Phosphorus: 0 mg

193. Raspberry Cucumber Smoothie

Preparation Time: 5 minutes
Cooking Time: 5 minutes
Servings: 2
INGREDIENTS:

- 1 cup fresh or frozen raspberries
- ½ cup English cucumber, diced
- 1 cup Homemade Rice Milk (or use unsweetened store-bought) or almond milk
- 2 tsp. chia seeds
- 1 tsp. honey
- 3 ice cubes

DIRECTIONS:

1. Place the raspberries, cucumber, rice milk, chia seeds, and honey in a blender. Then, blend until smooth.
2. Add the ice cubes. Then, blend until thick and smooth.
3. Pour into 2 tall glasses. Serve immediately.

NUTRITION:

- Calories: 125 kcal
- Fat: 1.1 g
- Carbs: 23.5 g
- Protein: 6 g
- Sodium: 44 mg
- Potassium: 199 mg
- Phosphorus: 54 mg

194. Sunny Pineapple Smoothie

Preparation Time: 5 minutes
Cooking Time: 5 minutes
Servings: 2
INGREDIENTS:

- ½ cup pineapple chunks, frozen
- ⅔ cup almond milk
- ½ tsp. ginger powder
- 1 tbsp. agave syrup

DIRECTIONS:

1. Prepare a blender and mix everything until nice and smooth (around 30 seconds).
2. Transfer into a tall glass or Mason jar.
3. Serve and enjoy.

NUTRITION:

- Calories: 144 kcal
- Fat: 0.36 g
- Carbs: 37 g
- Protein: 1.6 g
- Sodium: 354 mg

- Potassium: 1000 mg
- Phosphorus: 40 mg

195. Mango Cheesecake Smoothie

Preparation Time: 5 minutes
Cooking Time: 5 minutes
Servings: 2
INGREDIENTS:

- 1 cup Homemade Rice Milk
- ½ ripe fresh mango, peeled and chopped
- 2 tbsp. cream cheese, at room temperature
- 1 tsp. honey
- ½ vanilla bean split and seeds
- Pinch nutmeg, ground
- 3 ice cubes

DIRECTIONS:

1. Place the rice milk, mango, cream cheese, honey, vanilla bean seeds, and nutmeg in a blender, and blend until smooth and thick.
2. Add the ice cubes and blend.
3. Serve in two glasses immediately.

NUTRITION:

- Calories: 177 kcal
- Fat: 4 g
- Carbs: 10 g
- Protein: 24 g
- Sodium: 346 mg
- Potassium: 66 mg
- Phosphorus: 62 mg

196. Hot Cocoa

Preparation Time: 5 minutes
Cooking Time: 5 minutes
Servings: 1
INGREDIENTS:

- 1 tbsp. cocoa powder, unsweetened
- 2 tsp. Splenda granulated sugar
- 3 tbsp. whipped dessert topping
- 1 cup water, at room temperature
- 2 tbsp. water, cold

DIRECTIONS:

1. Prepare saucepan over medium heat and let it heat until hot.
2. Take a cup, place cocoa powder and sugar in it, pour in cold water, and mix well.
3. Then slowly stir in hot water until cocoa mixture dissolves and top with whipped topping.

4. Serve straight away.

NUTRITION:

- Calories: 120 kcal
- Fat: 3 g
- Carbs: 23 g
- Protein: 1 g
- Sodium: 110 mg
- Potassium: 199 mg
- Phosphorus: 88 mg

197. Rice Milk

Preparation Time: 2 minutes
Cooking Time: 2 minutes
Servings: 2
INGREDIENTS:

- 1 cup rice milk, unenriched, chilled
- 1 scoop vanilla whey protein

DIRECTIONS:

1. Pour milk in a blender, add whey protein, and then pulse until well blended.
2. Distribute the milk into 2 glasses and serve.

NUTRITION:

- Calories: 120 kcal
- Fat: 2 g
- Carbs: 24 g
- Protein: 0 g
- Sodium: 86 mg
- Potassium: 27 mg
- Phosphorus: 56 mg

198. Almond Milk

Preparation Time: 3 minutes
Cooking Time: 2 minutes
Servings: 3
INGREDIENTS:

- 1 cup almonds, soaked in warm water for 10 minutes
- 1 tsp. vanilla extract, unsweetened
- 3 cup water, filtered

DIRECTIONS:

1. Drain the soaked almonds, place them into the blender, pour in water, and blend for 2 minutes until almonds are chopped.
2. Strain the milk by passing it through cheesecloth into a bowl, discard almond meal, and then stir vanilla into the milk.

3. Cover the milk, refrigerate until chilled, and when ready to serve, stir it well, pour the milk evenly into the glasses and then serve.

NUTRITION:

- Calories: 30 kcal
- Fat: 2.5 g
- Carbs: 1 g
- Protein: 1 g
- Sodium: 170 mg
- Potassium: 140 mg
- Phosphorus: 30 mg

199. Cucumber and Lemon-Flavored Water

Preparation Time: 5 minutes
Cooking Time: 3 hours
Servings: 10
INGREDIENTS:

- 1 lemon, deseeded, sliced
- ¼ cup fresh mint leaves, chopped
- 1 medium cucumber, sliced
- ¼ cup fresh basil leaves, chopped
- 10 cups water

DIRECTIONS:

1. Place the papaya and mint in a large pitcher. Pour in the water.
2. Stir and place the pitcher in the refrigerator to infuse overnight if possible.
3. Serve cold.

NUTRITION:

- Calories: 10 kcal
- Fat: 0 g
- Carbs: 2.25 g
- Protein: 0.12 g
- Sodium: 2.5 mg
- Potassium: 8.9 mg
- Phosphorus: 10 mg

200. Blueberry Smoothie

Preparation Time: 5 minutes
Cooking Time: 2 minutes
Servings: 4
INGREDIENTS:

- 1 cup blueberries, frozen
- 6 tbsp. protein powder
- 8 packets Splenda
- 14 oz. apple juice, unsweetened
- 8 cubes ice

DIRECTIONS:

1. Take a blender and place all the ingredients (in order) in it. Process for 1 minute until smooth.
2. Distribute the smoothie between four glasses and then serve.

NUTRITION:

- Calories: 162 kcal
- Fat: 0.5 g
- Carbs: 30 g
- Protein: 8 g
- Sodium: 123.4 mg
- Potassium: 223 mg
- Phosphorus: 109 mg

201. Healthy Green Smoothie

Preparation Time: 5 minutes
Cooking Time: 5 minutes
Servings: 2
INGREDIENTS:

- 2 cups baby cabbage leaves, packed
- 1 stalk celery, cut in chunks
- 1 cucumber, peeled, and cut into chunks
- ½ to 1 cup water or ice

DIRECTIONS:

1. Place the cabbage, celery, and cucumber in a high-speed blender and blend until smooth.
2. Add the water or ice and blend.

NUTRITION:

- Calories: 132 kcal
- Fat: 3 g
- Carbohydrates: 14 g
- Protein: 6 g
- Sodium: 4 mg
- Potassium: 366 mg
- Phosphorus: 46 mg

202. Carrot Orange Ginger Smoothie

Preparation Time: 5 minutes
Cooking Time: 5 minutes
Servings: 2
INGREDIENTS:

- 2 tbsp. flax seeds, ground
- ½ cup coconut milk, unsweetened
- 2 oranges, peeled, sections separated and frozen
- 1-inch ginger, peeled and grated
- 2 large carrots, peeled, then cut into small chunks

DIRECTIONS:

1. Add the ginger and carrots, blending until smooth and creamy.
2. Pour in the coconut milk and frozen orange segments; pulse to mix until chunky.

NUTRITION:

- Calories: 112 kcal
- Fat: 0 g
- Carbohydrates: 27 g
- Protein: 0 g
- Sodium: 28 mg
- Potassium: 450 mg
- Phosphorus: 40 mg

203. Cherry Limeade Smoothie

Preparation Time: 5 minutes
Cooking Time: 5 minutes
Servings: 2
INGREDIENTS:

- 1 heaping cup cherries, frozen and pitted
- 1 ripe peach, peeled and sliced
- 1 tbsp. chia seeds, ground
- 1 cup almond milk
- 1 to 2 limes, juiced
- 1 handful ice

DIRECTIONS:

1. Add the cherries and peach slices to the blender and pulse.
2. Add the ground chia seeds and pulse.
3. Pour in the almond milk, lime juice, and ice, blend until smooth and thick.
4. Add ice if more thickness is needed.

NUTRITION:

- Calories: 130 kcal
- Fat: 0 g
- Carbohydrates: 32 g
- Protein: 1 g

204. Layered Smoothie

Preparation Time: 5 minutes
Cooking Time: 5 minutes
Servings: 2
INGREDIENTS:

- 1 ¼ cups mango pieces, frozen
- 1 cup almond milk, divided
- 2 tsp. stevia, 1 tbsp. agave syrup
- 1 cup strawberries, frozen, hulled and cut in half

- 1 cup fresh cabbage

DIRECTIONS:

1. Place the mango pieces in the blender, pour in a third of the milk, and add a third sweetener.
2. Process until smooth, then pour into the bottom of a large glass.
3. Place the strawberries in the blender along with another third of the milk and the sweetener; blend this until smooth. Pour gently over the mango layer in the glass.
4. Place the cabbage and the remaining milk and sweetener in the blender and blend until smooth. Pour on top of the strawberry layer.

NUTRITION:

- Calories: 408 kcal
- Fat: 3 g
- Carbohydrates: 94 g
- Protein: 9 g

205. Green Apple Orange Spice

Preparation Time: 5 minutes
Cooking Time: 5 minutes
Servings: 2
INGREDIENTS:

- 1 medium Granny Smith apple, cut into slices
- 1 cup orange juice
- 1 ½ cup kale
- 1 tsp. ginger root, peeled and minced
- 1 tbsp. chia or flaxseed, ground
- ½ tsp. cinnamon, ground

DIRECTIONS:

1. Place the apple in the blender and pulse to break it up.
2. Add the orange juice and pulse again to break up and roughly combine.
3. Add the kale and blend.
4. Add the gingerroot, chia, or flax seed and cinnamon, blend until smooth and thick.

NUTRITION:

- Calories: 200 kcal
- Fat: 1 g
- Carbohydrates: 16 g
- Protein: 1 g

206. Maple Fig Smoothie

Preparation Time: 10 minutes
Cooking Time: 5 minutes
Servings: 2

INGREDIENTS:

- ¾ cup oats rolled
- 1 cup preferred milk
- 6 to 8 figs, stemmed and cut in half
- 2 tbsp. almond, cashew, or peanut butter
- 1 pinch ginger, ground
- 1 pinch cinnamon
- 1 pinch cayenne pepper
- ¼ cup cocoa powder
- ¼ cup coconut oil
- ¼ cup maple syrup

DIRECTIONS:

1. Combine the oats and milk in the blender, pulse, and sit for about two minutes.
2. Add the nut butter, ginger, cinnamon, and cayenne pepper, blend until smooth.
3. In a bowl, combine the cocoa powder, coconut oil, and maple syrup. Whisk until thoroughly mixed, then pour most of it into the blender and blend until smooth and creamy.
4. Divide among individual glasses, drizzling the rest of the syrup on top as an artistic garnish.

NUTRITION:

- Calories: 304 kcal
- Fat: 12 g
- Carbohydrates: 46 g
- Protein: 8 g

207. Mint Protein: Smoothie

Preparation Time: 5 minutes
Cooking Time: 5 minutes
Servings: 2
INGREDIENTS:

- 1 tbsp. chia seeds, ground
- 1 tbsp. hemp seeds, ground
- 1 tbsp. flax seed, ground
- ½ cup mango pieces, frozen
- 1 large orange, peeled and sectioned
- 1 scoop vanilla protein powder
- ¾ cup coconut milk, unsweetened
- 5 to 6 fresh mint leaves

DIRECTIONS:

1. Grind the chia, hemp, and flaxseed and place them in a blender.
2. Add the frozen mango, the orange sections and pulse a few times.
3. Add the protein powder and coconut milk; pulse again to combine.

4. Add the mint leaves and blend until smooth.
5. Add some ice cubes if the smoothie is too runny. Blend again until thick and smooth.

NUTRITION:

- Calories: 120 kcal
- Fat: 2 g
- Carbohydrates: 4 g
- Protein: 20 g

208. Peachy Keen Smoothie

Preparation Time: 5 minutes
Cooking Time: 5 minutes
Servings: 2
INGREDIENTS:

- ½ cup almond milk, unsweetened (optional substitution: coconut milk)
- ¼ cup oats, rolled
- 1 tsp. chia seeds, ground
- 2 ripe peaches, pitted, skinned, and cut into slices
- ¼ cup fresh orange juice

DIRECTIONS:

1. Place the almond milk, rolled oats, and chia seeds in the blender and pulse a few times. Leave for 2–3 minutes.
2. Add the peaches, orange juice, and blend until smooth and creamy.
3. If you want to add sweetener, add it, and blend in.

NUTRITION:

- Calories: 170 kcal
- Fat: 1 g
- Carbohydrates: 35 g
- Protein: 9 g

209. Pear Basil Citrus Smoothie

Preparation Time: 5 minutes
Cooking Time: 5 minutes
Servings: 2
INGREDIENTS:

- 4 large stalks celery, juiced (only use the juice; discard the solids)
- 8 oz. pear, sliced
- ¼ cup lemon juice, fresh squeezed
- 1 cup fresh basil leaves

DIRECTIONS:

1. Juice the celery stalks and pour the juice into the blender.
2. Add the lemon juice and pear slices and blend until smooth.
3. Add the basil leaves and blend again until smooth.

4. If the smoothie appears runny, blend in ice a little at a time until it reaches your preferred consistency.

NUTRITION:

- Calories: 110 kcal
- Fat: 1 g
- Carbohydrates: 22 g
- Protein: 2 g

210. Chocolate Mint Smoothie

Preparation Time: 5 minutes
Cooking Time: 5 minutes
Servings: 2
INGREDIENTS:

- ¾ cup plain Greek Yogurt
- 1 cup almond milk
- ¼ cup fresh mint, tightly packed
- 1 cup baby cabbage leaves
- 1 tbsp. maple syrup
- ¼ cup semi-sweet chocolate chips
- 2 cups ice

DIRECTIONS:

1. Place the yogurt, milk, mint, and cabbage in a blender and blend on high until frothy.
2. Add the maple syrup and chocolate chips and blend for a few seconds to break up the chocolate chips.
3. Add the ice and blend until thick and smooth.

NUTRITION:

- Calories: 129 kcal
- Fat: 11 g
- Carbohydrates: 3 g
- Protein: 5 g

PUDDINGS AND CAKES

211. Vegan Chocolate Peanut Butter Cheesecake

Preparation Time: 15 minutes
Cooking Time: 20-30 minutes
Servings: 4-6
INGREDIENTS:
For the base:

- 3 ½ oz. dates
- 3 ½ oz. raisins
- 3 ½ oz. sunflower seeds
- 1 ½ oz. walnuts
- 3 ½ oz. peanuts

Filling:

- ½ lb. tofu
- 3 ½ oz. cocoa
- 3 ½ oz. coconut oil
- 2 oz. Coconut milk
- Pinch salt

DIRECTIONS:

1. Process the dates, raisins, sunflower, walnuts, peanuts, and cocoa and assemble the cake base.
2. Spread with peanut butter. Blend the tofu, cocoa, coconut oil, 50 g of peanut butter, coconut milk, salt, and vanilla essence.
3. Decorate with melted chocolate.

NUTRITION:

- Calories: 197.7 kcal
- Protein: 2.6 g
- Fat: 10.3 g
- Carbohydrates: 25 g

212. Vegan Corn Cake

Preparation Time: 5 minutes
Cooking Time: 30-40 minutes
Servings: 5
INGREDIENTS:

- Vegan cake batter
- 1 small onion
- 1 small bell pepper
- Margarine, to taste
- 2 tbsp. cornstarch
- Soy milk to taste
- 2 cans yellow corn kernels
- Pepper
- Nutmeg

DIRECTIONS:

1. Chop the onion and the bell pepper and fry them in a saucepan with the margarine until soft.
2. Add the corn starch and mix well.
3. Incorporate the soy milk and continue cooking until a thick béchamel is formed.
4. Turn off the heat, season, and add the nutmeg.
5. Add the drained corn grains to the preparation and mix well.
6. Spread the tart dough in a tart pan and fill with the preparation. If the dough is bought, cover it with the other dough cover.
7. Add a little margarine or oil and take to a moderate oven until cooked.

NUTRITION:

- Calories: 67.1 kcal
- Protein: 1.8 g
- Fat: 0.6 g
- Carbohydrates: 15.2 g

213. Strawberry Biscuit Cake

Preparation Time: 15 minutes
Cooking Time: 30-40 minutes
Servings: 4
INGREDIENTS:

- 1 can milk, condensed
- ½ cup milk
- 4 egg yolks
- 1 tablet semi-bitter chocolate
- 1 pot cream
- ½ lb. cookies
- 1 cup whipping cream
- ½ lb. strawberries, sliced

DIRECTIONS:

1. Place the milk, condensed milk, and egg yolks over low heat, constantly stirring until thick. Cool for 1 hour.
2. In a bowl, mix the melted chocolate with the cream. Reserve.
3. On a platter, put the condensed milk mixture, a large number of cookies on top, then the chocolate mixture, the second portion of wafers, and cover with the whipping cream.
4. Finish the preparation with strawberry slices on top. Arrange in circular shapes.
5. Enjoy it!

NUTRITION:

- Calories: 90 kcal
- Protein: 2.3 g
- Fat: 2.7 g
- Carbohydrates: 15.3 g

214. Potato and Mushroom Cake

Preparation Time: 20 minutes
Cooking Time: 1 hour
Servings: 8
INGREDIENTS:

- 8 medium potatoes
- ½ lb. mushroom
- ½ lb. Portobello in thin sheets
- 1 cup gruyere, grated
- ½ cup Parmesan, grated
- 3 tbsp. parsley
- 1 tbsp. oregano
- ½ cup vegetable broth
- Salt, pepper, and nutmeg
- 1 tbsp. butter

DIRECTIONS:

1. Heat the oven to 360°F and grease a baking dish with a tbsp. of butter

2. Cut the potatoes and mushrooms into very thin sheets
3. In the greased refractory, make layers of potatoes, mushrooms, gruyere, seasoning between layers.
4. At the end, add the vegetable stock, cover with aluminum, and bake for 1h.
5. Uncover, cover with cheese, and gratin with Parmesan until golden.

NUTRITION:

- Calories: 117.5 kcal
- Protein: 2.9 g
- Fat: 3.2 g
- Carbohydrates: 20.2 g

215. Azteca Cake

Preparation Time: 15 minutes
Cooking Time: 30-40 minutes
Servings: 2
INGREDIENTS:

- 1 lb. chicken supreme, shredded
- 5 chilies from heaven
- 2 garlic cloves
- 1 onion
- 3 cups water
- 8 wheat tortillas
- 1 cup corn kernels
- ½ cup cream
- 2 tbsp. coriander, chopped
- 1 ½ cup mozzarella or cheese of preference
- Salt oil

DIRECTIONS:

1. Heat the chilies, garlic, and onion with 3 cups of water.
2. Boil 10 minutes. Move to a blender and process with the same cooking juice.
3. Strain and reserve the sauce.
4. Brown the tortillas in oil and reserve. Dip it in the sauce and arrange in the base of an ovenproof dish.
5. Sprinkle a little shredded chicken, some corn kernels, a little chili sauce, cream, and coriander.
6. Repeat this operation until you finish with all the ingredients.
7. Gratin in the oven at 400°F until the cheese is gratin.

NUTRITION:

- Calories: 140 kcal
- Protein: 11 g
- Fat: 12 g
- Carbohydrates: 10 g

216. Carrot and Tofu Cake

Preparation Time: 15 minutes
Cooking Time: 40 minutes
Servings: 4
INGREDIENTS:

- ½ lb. raw carrots, peeled and grated
- ½ lb. silky tofu
- ½ cup sunflower oil
- ½ lb. flour
- ½ lb. brown sugar
- 4 tsp. (1 sachet) chemical yeast
- 4 eggs
- 1 tsp. baking soda
- 1 tsp. cinnamon

DIRECTIONS:

1. Crush the carrots together with the oil and reserve. Sift together the dry ingredients (flour, yeast, baking soda, and cinnamon).
2. Beat the sugar in a bowl with the eggs until they are frothy.
3. Add the tofu and continue beating to integrate. Add the carrot, mix, and then dry ingredients twice, mixing well.
4. Pour into a 24 cm mold previously greased and floured. Take to the oven preheated to 360°F for about 40 minutes. To know if the cake is ready, click with a toothpick in the center. It is already cooked if it comes out clean.
5. Take it from the oven, let it cool in the mold, and then unmold.

NUTRITION:

- Calories: 133.5 kcal
- Protein: 4.3 g
- Fat: 3.7 g
- Carbohydrates: 23.7 g

217. Carrot Cake

Preparation Time: 15 minutes
Cooking Time: 45 minutes
Servings: 4

INGREDIENTS:

- 3 cups flour
- 2 tsp. cinnamon, ground
- 2 tsp. baking powder
- 1 tsp. baking soda
- 1 tsp. salt
- 1 ¼ cups vegetable oil
- ¾ cup sugar-free and fat-free applesauce
- 1 tsp. vanilla extract
- 2 cups carrots, crumbled
- 1 pineapple, drained and chopped
- 1 cup walnuts, chopped
- 1 cup vegan butter, softened

DIRECTIONS:

1. Preheat oven to 360°F and grease three 8-inch round cake pans with non-stick spray.
2. In a large bowl, beat together flour, cinnamon, baking powder, baking soda, and salt.
3. In a small bowl, oil, applesauce, and vanilla.
4. Add the egg mixture into the flour mixture until combined. Fold the carrots, pineapple, and walnuts.
5. Evenly distribute the dough between the prepared pans and bake in the oven for about 45 minutes. Let cool.
6. Prepare and beat butter in a bowl on medium-low speed until smooth and creamy, about 3 minutes. Whisk over medium until light and fluffy, scraping bowl as needed.
7. Remove the cooled cakes from their cans. Place one of the layers on a flat plate or cake stand.
8. Cover with ¾ cup of frosting. Put another layer of cake. Cover with ¾ cup of frosting. Place with the final layer of cake. Cover the cake with the remaining topping using a spatula.
9. Garnish with chopped walnuts along the bottom edge of the sides. Enjoy!

NUTRITION:

- Calories: 133.5 kcal
- Protein: 4.3 g
- Fat: 3.7 g
- Carbohydrates: 23.7 g

218. Orange and Chocolate Cake

Preparation Time: 30 minutes
Cooking Time: 45 minutes
Servings: 2
INGREDIENTS:
For the Cake:

- 3 cups flour
- 2 cups vegan butter
- 2 tsp. baking powder

- 2 cups sugar
- A pinch salt
- 2 ½ tbsp. orange zest
- 1 ½ tbsp. lemon zest
- 1 ½ cups orange juice.

For the filling:

- 1 cup sugar
- 2 ½ tbsp. flour
- 1 cup orange juice
- 2 tbsp. butter

DIRECTIONS:

1. Beat the butter, orange zest, lemon, and sugar.
2. Add flour, baking powder, and salt, alternating with the orange juice.
3. Flour and butter 2 molds of the same size. Distribute the mixture evenly in the two molds and bake for 45 minutes. Unmold and let cool.
4. For the filling, in a saucepan, mix the sugar, flour, orange juice, and yolks. Heat over low heat and stir until it boils slightly and thickens.
5. Take it from heat, add the butter, and let cool.
6. Put one layer of cake, filling, the other layer of cake, and more filling.

NUTRITION:

- Calories: 168.1 kcal
- Protein: 3.1 g
- Fat: 11.9 g
- Carbohydrates: 13.8 g

219. Tofu and Chocolate Mousse

Preparation Time: 20 minutes
Cooking Time: 5-10 minutes
Servings: 3
INGREDIENTS:

- 3 ½ oz. dark chocolate
- 4 oz. silky tofu at room temperature, strained

- 2 tbsp. maple syrup (can be replaced with honey, stevia, or corn syrup)

DIRECTIONS:

1. Melt the chocolate in the microwave at intervals of 30 seconds, mixing it between one and the other until it is completely melted.
2. Let warm. Beat the tofu with the syrup until it is creamy. Add the chocolate and continue beating until integrated. Serve in glasses and let stand in the fridge for 2 or 3 hours before serving.
3. You can accompany it with fresh fruit, grated chocolate, nuts, etc.

NUTRITION:

- Calories: 109.6 kcal
- Protein: 3.4 g
- Fat: 5.6 g
- Carbohydrates: 11.9 g

220. Vegan Chocolate Pudding

Preparation Time: 10 minutes
Cooking Time: 45 minutes
Servings: 2-4
INGREDIENTS:

- 2 cups organic wheat flour
- 1 tbsp. baking powder
- ½ cup organic cocoa
- 1 cup oil
- 1 cup organic sugar
- Zest of 1 orange
- Pinch salt
- Juice of 1 orange
- 1 cup vegan milk

DIRECTIONS:

1. Mix the sugar and the oil.
2. Add the vegan milk and continue mixing.
3. Add the pinch of salt, zest, and orange juice.
4. Sift the dry ones and incorporate them with an enveloping movement.
5. Cook in an oven at 170°C until a toothpick is inserted and it comes out moist.

NUTRITION:

- Calories: 197.7 kcal
- Protein: 2.6 g
- Fat: 10.3 g
- Carbohydrates: 25 g

221. Spice Cake

Preparation Time: 10 minutes
Cooking Time: 50 Minutes
Servings: 6
INGREDIENTS:

- 1 sweet potato, cooked and peeled
- ½ cup applesauce, unsweetened
- ½ cup almond milk
- ¼ cup maple syrup, pure
- 1 tsp. vanilla extract, pure
- 2 cups whole wheat flour
- ½ tsp. cinnamon, ground
- ½ tsp. baking soda
- ¼ tsp. ginger, ground

DIRECTIONS:

1. Ready your oven to 350°F, and then get a large bowl out. Mash your sweet potatoes, and then mix in the vanilla, milk, and maple syrup. Mix well.
2. Stir in the baking soda, cinnamon, flour, and ginger. Mix well.
3. Pour this batter into a baking dish that's been lined with parchment paper. Bake the batter for forty-five minutes.
4. Allow it to cool before slicing to serve.

NUTRITION:

- Calories: 220 kcal
- Fat: 14 g
- Carbohydrates: 40 g
- Protein: 5 g

222. Lemon Cake

Preparation Time: 10 minutes
Cooking Time: 5 hours and 10 minutes
Servings: 10
INGREDIENTS:
Crust:

- 1 cup dates, pitted
- 2 tbsp. maple syrup
- 2 ½ cups pecans

Filling:

- 1 lemon, juiced and zested
- ¾ cup maple syrup
- 1 ½ cups pineapple, crushed
- 3 cups cauliflower rice, prepared
- 3 avocados, halved and pitted
- ½ tsp. vanilla extract, pure
- ½ tsp. lemon extract
- 1 pinch cinnamon

Topping:

- 1 tsp. vanilla extract, pure
- 1 ½ cups coconut yogurt, plain
- 3 tbsp. maple syrup

DIRECTIONS:

1. Get a 9-inch springform pan out, lining it with parchment paper.
2. Put your pecans in a food processor, grinding until fine. Stir in the maple syrup and dates, blending for a minute more. Spread this into your pan to make the crust.
3. Blend your maple syrup, pineapple, lemon juice, lemon zest, cauliflower rice, and avocados in a food processor. Add in the lemon extract, cinnamon, and vanilla. Mix well.
4. Top your crust with this mixture and freeze for 5 hours.
5. To make your topping whisk all ingredients together, spreading it over your prepared cake.

NUTRITION:

- Calories: 142 kcal
- Fat: 8 g
- Carbohydrates: 0 g
- Protein: 0 g

223. Green Tea Pudding

Preparation Time: 10 minutes
Cooking Time: 1 hour
Servings: 2
INGREDIENTS:

- ½ cup coconut milk
- 1 and ½ cup avocado, pitted and peeled
- 1 tbsp. green tea powder
- 1 tsp. lime zest, grated
- 1 tbsp. sugar

DIRECTIONS:

1. Mix coconut milk with avocado, tea powder, lime zest, and sugar in your slow cooker.
2. Mix, place cover and cook on low for 1 hour.

3. Divide into cups and serve cold.

NUTRITION:

- Calories: 107 kcal
- Fat: 5 g
- Fiber: 3 g
- Carbohydrates: 6 g
- Protein: 8 g

224. Dates and Rice Pudding

Preparation Time: 10 minutes
Cooking Time: 3 hours
Servings: 2
INGREDIENTS:

- 1 cup dates, chopped
- ½ cup white rice
- 1 cup almond milk
- 1 tbsp. brown sugar
- 1 tsp. almond extract

DIRECTIONS:

1. In your slow cooker, mix the rice with the milk and the other ingredients, whisk, close and cook on Low for 3 hours.
2. Divide the pudding into bowls and serve.

NUTRITION:

- Calories: 152 kcal
- Fat: 5 g
- Fiber: 2 g
- Carbohydrates: 6 g
- Protein: 3 g

225. Chocolate and Avocado Mousse

Preparation Time: 40 minutes
Cooking Time: 5 minutes
Servings: 5

INGREDIENTS:

- 8 oz. (227 g) dark chocolate (60% cocoa or higher), chopped
- ¼ cup coconut milk, unsweetened
- 2 tbsp. coconut oil
- 2 ripe avocados, deseeded

DIRECTIONS:

1. Put the chocolate in a saucepan. Add the coconut milk and coconut oil.
2. Cook for 3 minutes or until the chocolate and coconut oil melt. Stir constantly.
3. Put the avocado in a food processor and melted chocolate. Pulse to combine until smooth.
4. Pour the mixture in a serving bowl, then sprinkle with salt. Refrigerate to chill for 30 minutes and serve.

NUTRITION:

- Calories: 654 kcal
- Fat: 46.8 g
- Protein: 7.2 g

226. Cool Avocado Pudding

Preparation Time: 3 hours
Cooking Time: 0 minute
Servings: 4
INGREDIENTS:

- 1 cup almond milk
- 2 avocados, peeled and pitted
- ¾ cup cocoa powder
- 1 tsp. vanilla extract
- 2 tbsp. Stevia
- ¼ tsp. cinnamon
- Walnuts, chopped

DIRECTIONS:

1. Arrange avocados in a blender and process well.
2. Put the cocoa powder, almond milk, Stevia, vanilla bean extract and mix well
3. Transfer into serving bowls and top with walnuts
4. Chill for 2-3 hours and serve!

NUTRITION:

- Calories: 221 kcal
- Fat: 8 g
- Protein: 3 g

227. Mango Coconut Cheesecake

Preparation Time: 4 hours and 10 minutes
Cooking Time: 0 minute
Servings: 4
INGREDIENTS:
For the Crust:

- 1 cup macadamia nuts
- 1 cup dates, pitted, soaked in hot water for 10 minutes

For the Filling:

- 2 cups cashews, set in warm water for 10 minutes
- ½ cup and 1 tbsp. maple syrup
- ⅓ cup and 2 tbsp. coconut oil
- ¼ cup lemon juice
- ½ cup and 2 tbsp. coconut milk, unsweetened, chilled

For the Topping:

- 1 cup fresh mango slices

DIRECTIONS:

1. Prepare the crust and, for this, put the walnuts in a food processor and blend until the mixture resembles crumbs.
2. Drain the dates, attach them to the food processor and blend for 2 minutes until thick.
3. Take a 4-inch cheesecake, put the date mixture in it, spread and press evenly, and set aside.
4. Prepare the filling and for this, put all the ingredients in a food processor and blend until the mixture is smooth.
5. Pour the filling into the crust, distribute evenly, and freeze for 4 hours until solidified.
6. Cover the cake with mango slices and then serve.

NUTRITION:

- Calories: 200 kcal
- Fat: 11 g
- Carbohydrates: 22.5 g
- Protein: 2 g
- Fiber: 1 g

228. Coconut Chia Pudding

Preparation Time: 15 minutes
Cooking Time: 30 minutes
Servings: 4
INGREDIENTS:

- 1 lime, juiced, and zested
- 14 oz. coconut milk, canned
- 2 dates
- 2 tbsp. chia seeds, ground
- 2 tsp. matcha powder

DIRECTIONS:

1. Get out a blender and blend everything until smooth.
2. Chill for 20 minutes before serving.

NUTRITION:

- Calories: 100 kcal
- Fat: 5.1 g
- Carbohydrates: 11.8 g
- Protein: 4.2 g
- Fiber: 3.1 g

229. Avocado Blueberry Cheesecake

Preparation Time: 15 minutes
Cooking Time: 1 hour 25 minutes
Servings: 8
INGREDIENTS:
Crust:

- 1 cup oats, rolled
- 1 cup walnuts
- 1 tsp. lime zest
- 1 cup dates, soft pitted

Filling:

- 2 tbsp. maple syrup
- 1 cup blueberries, frozen
- 2 avocados, peeled and pitted
- 2 tbsp. basil, fresh and minced fine
- 4 tbsp. lime juice

DIRECTIONS:

1. Pulse all crust ingredients together in your food processor, and then press into a pie pan.
2. Prepare all filling ingredients and blend until smooth. Then pour it into the crust.
3. Smooth out and freeze for 2 hours before serving.

NUTRITION:

- Calories: 73 kcal
- Fat: 4 g
- Protein: 2 g
- Carbohydrates: 8 g
- Fiber: 2 g

230. <u>**Mango Coconut Pudding**</u>

Preparation Time: 10 minutes
Cooking Time: 50 minutes
Servings: 4
INGREDIENTS:

- 1 cup coconut, shredded
- 1 cup coconut cream
- 1 mango, peeled and chopped
- 1 cup coconut milk
- 2 tbsp. coconut sugar
- 1 tsp. vanilla extract
- ½ tsp. cinnamon powder

DIRECTIONS:

1. In a pan, mix the coconut with the cream and the other ingredients, stir, simmer for 50 minutes over medium heat, divide into bowls and serve cold.

NUTRITION:

- Calories: 251 kcal
- Fat: 3.6 g
- Fiber: 4 g
- Carbohydrates: 16 g
- Protein: 7.1 g

ALTERNATIVE INFUSIONS AND HERBAL TEAS

231. Peppermint Tea

Preparation Time: 5 minutes
Cooking Time: 5–10 minutes
Servings: 1
INGREDIENTS:

- 1 tsp. peppermint leaves, dried
- 1 tsp. honey
- 1 cup water

DIRECTIONS:

1. Add 1 serving of peppermint in your tea strainer for each cup of tea you want.
2. Let the leaves in hot water for 5-10 minutes.
3. Add some sugar or honey, or you can drink it unsweetened as desired
4. Serve and enjoy.

General Benefits of this Tea:
Peppermint soothes heartburn and respiratory problems as a part of the mint family.

NUTRITION:

- Calories: 2.52 kcal
- Fat: 0.03 g
- Carbs: 0.48 g
- Protein: 0.12 g

232. Lavender Tea

Preparation Time: 5 minutes
Cooking Time: 5 minutes
Servings: 1
INGREDIENTS:

- 2 tsp. organic lavender, dried
- ¼ cup mint, dried
- 3 cups hot water
- 2 tsp. honey

DIRECTIONS:

1. Combine mint and lavender in a teapot.
2. Leave at least 5 minutes to be steep.
3. Using a tea strainer, pour tea into cups and add fresh lemon and honey.
4. Serve and enjoy.

General Benefits of this Tea:
Ancient cultures prized lavender because of its intoxicating scent and ability to relax the digestive tract, bringing restful sleep, and relieve depression. Lavender tea helps reduce respiratory problems, cough, asthma, bronchitis, and body temperature and is used to treat fever.

NUTRITION:

- Calories: 32 kcal
- Fat: 0 g
- Carbs: 9 g
- Protein: 0 g

233. Rose chamomile Tea

Preparation Time: 5 minutes
Cooking Time: 5 minutes
Servings: 1
INGREDIENTS:

- 2 cups rose petals
- 4 cups chamomile blossoms
- 2 cups lemongrass
- 1 tsp. honey

DIRECTIONS:

1. Put all ingredients thoroughly and keep them in a tightly sealed container.
2. Add 1 tsp. of the mixture to a cup of water with a tea strainer.
3. Add some honey or drink it unsweetened as desired.
4. Serve and enjoy.

General Benefits of this Tea:
Roses are a rich source of vitamins. You get an excellent nerve tonic when you mix rose petals with the relaxing properties of chamomile.

NUTRITION:

- Calories: 0 kcal
- Fat: 0 g
- Carbs: 0 g
- Protein: 0 g

234. Hibiscus Green Tea

Preparation Time: 5 minutes
Cooking Time: 5 minutes
Servings: 1
INGREDIENTS:

- 6 tsp. green tea
- ½ tsp. hibiscus blooms
- 2 oz. fruit or berries, dried
- 2 tsp. honey

DIRECTIONS:

1. Mix the ingredients well and add sugar to taste.
2. Add in a quart of boiling water and let it steep for up to 3 minutes.
3. Strain herbs and discard them.
4. Serve and enjoy.

General Benefits of this Tea:

Hibiscus flowers are loaded with powerful antioxidants and help in the reduction of cholesterol and reduce excess weight. This tea will reduce systolic blood pressure and hypertension and lower blood pressure for type–2 diabetes.

NUTRITION:

- Calories: 25 kcal
- Fat: 0 g
- Carbs: 6 g
- Protein: 0 g

235. Flax Seed Tea

Preparation Time: 5 minutes
Cooking Time: 3 hours and 10 minutes
Servings:
INGREDIENTS:

- 1 tsp. flaxseed powder
- 3 no's cloves
- 1 pinch cinnamon powder
- 2 cups water
- 2 tsp. honey

DIRECTIONS:

1. Add 1 tsp. of finely ground flaxseed in a cup of cold water.
2. Leave it for 3 hours and mix it occasionally.
3. Boil it for 10 minutes.
4. Add the cinnamon powder, cloves in the boiling water.
5. Strain the herbs through a strainer.
6. Add honey as desired.
7. Serve and enjoy.

General Benefits of this Tea:

Flax tea contains a rich source of omega-3 fatty acids and soluble and insoluble fibers. It is very effective in removing toxins from our intestinal tract. It reduces dryness and flakiness and improves symptoms of acne, eczema, skin allergies, and sunburn. It lowers cholesterol and improves heart health.

NUTRITION:

- Calories: 55 kcal
- Fat: 4 g
- Carbs: 3 g
- Protein: 1 g

236. Basil Leaves Tea

Preparation Time: 5 minutes
Cooking Time: 5–10 minutes
Servings: 1
INGREDIENTS:

- 5 no's basil leaves
- 1 cup water
- 3 tsp. honey

DIRECTIONS:

1. Add basil leaves to the teapot.
2. Let it steep for 5-10 minutes.
3. Strain the leaves through a strainer.
4. Add honey as desired.
5. Serve and enjoy.

General Benefits of this Tea:

Basil Leaves act as an adaptogen. It is a natural substance that allows your body to adapt to stress and promotes mental balance. Basil contains pharmacological properties to help your mind cope with many types of stress.

NUTRITION:

- Calories: 1.38 kcal
- Fat: 0.03 g
- Carbs: 0.15 g
- Protein: 0.18 g

237. Guava Tea

Preparation Time: 5 minutes
Cooking Time:
Servings: 1
INGREDIENTS:

- 6 no's guava leaves
- 2 cups water
- ½ tsp. fenugreek
- 3 tsp. honey

DIRECTIONS:

1. Add 2 cups of water and make it boil.
2. Add Guava Leaves and Fenugreek in the boiling water.
3. Let it steep for 10 minutes.
4. Strain the leaves through a strainer.
5. Add honey as desired.
6. Serve and enjoy.

General Benefits of this Tea:

Guava is effective in preventing and treating swollen gums and toothache. It helps lower cholesterol, keeps the heart and vascular tissues healthy, cleanses the digestive tract, and reduces abdominal pain and diarrhea.

NUTRITION:

- Calories: 0 kcal
- Fat: 0 g
- Carbs: 1 g
- Protein: 0 g

238. Ginger Onion Tea

Preparation Time: 5 minutes
Cooking Time: 10–15 minutes
Servings: 1
INGREDIENTS:

- 2 small onions
- 2-inch pieces ginger
- 2 cups water
- 3 tsp. honey

DIRECTIONS:

1. Add 2 cups of water and make it boil.
2. Add chopped onion and ginger to the boiling water.
3. Let it steep for 10-15 minutes.
4. Strain the herbs through a strainer.
5. Add honey as desired.
6. Serve and enjoy.

General Benefits of this Tea:

This tea enables the proper functioning of the liver, increases appetite, increases immunity power, and helps fight against respiratory tract problems.

NUTRITION:

- Calories: 7 kcal
- Fat: 0 g
- Carbs: 2 g
- Protein: 0.1 g

239. Turmeric Tea

Preparation Time: 5 minutes
Cooking Time: 10–15 minutes
Servings: 1
INGREDIENTS:

- 2 tsp. turmeric
- 1 tsp. cinnamon powder
- 3 no's cloves
- A pinch nutmeg
- ½ tsp. black pepper
- 2 cups water
- 3 tsp. honey

DIRECTIONS:

1. Add 2 cups of water and make it boil.
2. Add chopped all the ingredients in the boiling water except honey.
3. Let it steep for 10-15 minutes.
4. Strain the herbs through a strainer.
5. Add honey as desired.
6. Serve and enjoy.

General Benefits of this Tea:

This tea has a powerful soothing remedy and has many healing properties. It supports digestion, immune, and liver function, and it has anti-inflammatory and anti-cancer properties. It is used in traditional medicines as a treatment for many digestive conditions.

NUTRITION:

- Calories: 8 kcal
- Fat: 0 g
- Carbs: 1 g
- Protein: 0 g

240. Poppy Seeds Tea

Preparation Time: 5 minutes
Cooking Time: 10 minutes
Servings: 1
INGREDIENTS:

- 1.5 tsp. poppy seeds
- 3 no's cloves
- 1 tsp. cardamom powder
- 2 cups water
- 2 tsp. honey

DIRECTIONS:

1. Add all the ingredients to boiling water.
2. Let it steep for 10 minutes.
3. Strain the herbs through a strainer.
4. Add honey as desired.
5. Serve and enjoy.

General Benefits of this Tea:

This tea helps to have a deep and peaceful sleep. Increase appetite and increase productivity. This tea helps to proper blood flow in nerves.

NUTRITION:

- Calories: 46 kcal
- Fat: 3 g
- Carbs: 2 g
- Protein: 1 g

241. Elderflower Tea

Preparation Time: 5 minutes
Cooking Time: 10 minutes
Servings: 1
INGREDIENTS:

- 2 tsp. elderflower, dried
- 1 cup water
- 3 tsp. honey

DIRECTIONS:

1. Bring the water to a boil
2. Pour water over elderflower petals Cover and steep for 10 minutes
3. Put some honey or sugar to taste if desired.
4. Strain through a strainer into the teacup and add honey.
5. Serve and enjoy.

General Benefit of this tea:

This tea support heart health, improves antioxidant status and has a variety of anti-cancer, anti-diabetes, and anti-inflammatory effects.

NUTRITION:

- Calories: 0 kcal
- Fat: 0 g
- Carbs: 0 g
- Protein: 0 g

242. Hibiscus Raspberry Green Tea

Preparation Time: 5 minutes
Cooking Time: 3 minutes
Servings: 1
INGREDIENTS:

- 6 tsp. green tea
- 6 tsp. chamomile
- ½ cup hibiscus flower, dried
- 1-2 oz. raspberries, dried
- 3 tsp. honey

DIRECTIONS:

1. Blend all together in a mason jar.

2. Store in an airtight container to avoid sunlight.
3. Add 4-6 tsp. to make one quart of tea if you will make it iced. (1 Tsp. for Hot tea).
4. Steep for 3 minutes.
5. Strain the herbs through a strainer.
6. Add honey as desired.
7. Serve cold and enjoy.

General Benefits of this tea:

This tea helps lower blood pressure and blood fat levels, and it also boosts liver health, promotes weight loss.

NUTRITION:

- Calories: 0 kcal
- Fat: 0 g
- Carbs: 0 g
- Protein: 0 g

243. Fennel Tea

Preparation Time: 5 minutes
Cooking Time: 30 minutes
Servings: 1
INGREDIENTS:

- 1 tsp. fennel seeds
- 1 cup water
- 2 tsp. honey

DIRECTIONS:

1. Take 1 tsp. of fennel seeds and soak in warm water for 30 minutes.
2. Now, crush the fennel seeds within the same water used to soak the fennel seeds.
3. Boil the water with crushed fennel seeds.
4. Strain the seeds through a strainer.
5. Add honey as desired.
6. Serve and enjoy.

General Benefits of this Tea:

Fennel Tea can do wonders for the respiratory, gastrointestinal, and immune systems while also providing antioxidant, antibacterial, antispasmodic, and anti-inflammatory effects.

NUTRITION:

- Calories: 7 kcal
- Fat: 0 g
- Carbs: 1 g
- Protein: 0 g

244. Blackberry Tea

Preparation Time: 5 minutes
Cooking Time: 5–10 minutes
Servings: 1
INGREDIENTS:

- 2 tsp. blackberry leaves, dried
- 1 cup water
- 3 tsp. honey

DIRECTIONS:

1. Boil 1 cup of water.
2. Place 2 tsp. of dried blackberry leaves in a bowl.
3. Let it steep for 5-10 minutes.
4. Serve and enjoy.

General Benefits of this Tea:

Blackberry Tea can be useful to stimulate the cognitive function of the brain and also sharpen memory. Blackberry tea will protect the heart and bones, boost our immune system, and helps to treat blood clotting.

NUTRITION:

- Calories: 0 kcal
- Fat: 0 g
- Carbs: 0 g
- Protein: 0 g

245. Luscious Lemon Tea

Preparation Time: 5 minutes
Cooking Time: 10 minutes
Servings: 1
INGREDIENTS:

- ¼ cup lemon balm
- ¾ cup lemongrass
- 1 ½ tsp. honey

DIRECTIONS:

1. Put all the ingredients well in a glass container.
2. Add in hot water and let the tea steep for up to 10 minutes.
3. You can add natural sweetener or honey as desired.
4. Serve and enjoy.

General Benefits of this Tea:

Lemon is a favorite addition to natural herbal tea, and it has Vitamin C and other helpful vitamins. Take a sip of this lemony tea when you wake up in the morning.

NUTRITION:

- Calories: 0 kcal
- Fat: 0 g
- Carbs: 1 g
- Protein: 0 g

246. Morning Turmeric Tonic

Preparation Time: 10 minutes
Cooking Time: 5 minutes
Servings: 2
INGREDIENTS:

- 2 cups hot water (not boiling)
- 2 tsp. turmeric powder
- 1 lemon, sliced
- 3-4 peppercorns
- 1 inch ginger, grated

DIRECTIONS:

1. In a mortar, put in the turmeric, peppercorns, and ginger and give it a good grind using a pestle to create a paste
2. Divide the paste evenly into the serving cups or mugs, put in slices of lemon, pour hot water. Stir and serve.

NUTRITION:

- Calories: 8 kcal
- Fat: 0 g
- Carbs: 1 g
- Protein: 0 g

247. Licorice Tea for Energy Boost

Preparation Time: 10 minutes
Cooking Time: 5 minutes
Servings: 2
INGREDIENTS:

- 1 tsp. fresh licorice root
- Licorice tea
- 1 tsp. peppermint tea, dried
- Handful fresh peppermint small
- 1-2 tsp. rooibos tea

DIRECTIONS:

1. Prepare 2 cups of water in a small pot, then let it boil, put all the ingredients in.
2. Let steep for 3 to 4 minutes.
3. Strain and serve.

NUTRITION:

- Calories: 0 kcal
- Fat: 0 g
- Carbs: 1 g
- Protein: 0 g

248. Stress Relief Tea

Preparation Time: 20 minutes
Cooking Time: 5 minutes
Servings: 2
INGREDIENTS:

- 2 tsp. holy basil, dried
- 1 tsp. lemon balm, dried
- 1 tsp. chamomile, dried
- ½ tsp. lavender, dried
- ½ tsp. eleuthero, root dried

DIRECTIONS:

1. Put all the ingredients in a glass cup and add hot water.
2. Cover the cup and let steep for 20 minutes.
3. Strain tea into another cup. Add sweetener or honey if desired, and enjoy!

NUTRITION:

- Calories: 0 kcal
- Fat: 0 g
- Carbs: 1 g
- Protein: 0 g

249. Powerhouse Green Tea

Preparation Time: 20 minutes
Cooking Time: 5 minutes
Servings: 2
INGREDIENTS:

- 1 tsp. rosehip, dried
- 1 tsp. chamomile flowers
- 1 tsp. green tea
- 1 tsp. hibiscus, dried

DIRECTIONS:

1. In a small pot, prepare 2 cups of water, boil it, and add all the ingredients.
2. Let it steep for 3 to 4 minutes. Strain and serve.

NUTRITION:

- Calories: 0 kcal
- Fat: 0 g
- Carbs: 1 g
- Protein: 0 g

250. Lemon Ginger Tea

Preparation Time: 10 minutes
Cooking Time: 5 minutes
Servings: 2
INGREDIENTS:

- 1 tsp. plain tea
- 1 tsp. honey
- ¼ lemon, sliced
- ½ tsp. cinnamon, ground
- 1-inch fresh ginger, sliced or grated

DIRECTIONS:

1. Prepare 2 cups of water in a small pot, let it boil, then put all the ingredients in.
2. Let steep for 5 to 6 minutes. Make fresh and enjoy immediately.

NUTRITION:

- Calories: 0 kcal
- Fat: 0 g
- Carbs: 1 g
- Protein: 0 g

The right approach to a healthy diet is getting a balanced proportion of all necessary nutrients. Balanced diets are not meant for people with healthy kidneys alone, and it is possible to get meals having all the vital body requirements even when you are on a specific nutrient restriction therapy. A balanced renal-healthy meal should have the right proportion of calories, proteins, vegetables, fruits, and water. As you know, they have their specific roles in ensuring that the kidneys remain healthy.

Meal planning involves including these in a single serving of food. The point of emphasis is that food should be enjoyed, even when you may have to let go of some things. There are essentials to successful meal planning. The following are some generally useful tips:

- Have an objective

Why are you planning your meals? In this case, the goal is to have healthier kidneys. Your overall aim may be broken down into measurable aims to assess how you are doing.

- A handy knowledge of what you need

Equip yourself with the pros and cons of the renal diet so that there are no blurred lines.

Although you may not need to make regular visits to a dietician at this stage, it will be good to have one look over the meal plan.

There may need to make additions or subtractions. Emphasis is on individuality in this plan. Therefore, your dietician may need to go over the plan to ensure it is tailored to meet your specific needs. If you don't have one, consult your doctor.

- Be open-minded

There may be restrictions that make you unhappy but bear in mind that this is not for nothing. The little inconvenience can't be compared with the healthy results.

- Be flexible with your plans

It is good to have interchangeable alternatives when planning meals.

- Work with your budget

What is the essence of organizing what you will eat if you stress yourself over the money? Work on a diet based on your financial capability.

- Meal planning is not without its benefits

It helps to maximize time, resources, and money.

You can reason thoroughly on the menu with meal planning, putting whatever is available into good use, and minimizing wastage. There is no rush, and you are relaxed. You also end up saving yourself some energy because everything is organized.

- Planning your meals puts a personal touch on it

It gives you gratification and a sense of belonging. It does feel good to do something meaningful for oneself, especially when the news of chronic kidney disease is taking its toll on your emotions.

- Helps in creating colorful, delicious, and appealing meals

Eating goes beyond just having to put something in the stomach, and it should come with a satisfaction that is more than just killing your hunger.

- It helps in adherence

Dieting needs discipline. When you think about the food or edibles you need to do without, you may get tempted to ditch everything and throw caution to the wind.

- It takes care of the craving

You may feel the desire to binge on some forbidden foods at times. However, a handy meal menu from adequate planning makes it easier to curb it and go with what you have. Sometimes, excessive hunger is what leads to bingeing. When you feel hungry, and there is nothing to satisfy it, your body changes, secreting hormones that heighten the sense of hunger so much that you will eat the available food if there is no control.

- Meal planning curbs extravagant spending during shopping

You know what you need. Therefore, your trip to the grocery yields only the essentials and unnecessary stuff, something most people find difficult to do.

Days	Breakfast	Lunch	Dinner
1	Apple Cherry Breakfast Risotto	Lettuce Wraps with Chicken	Cilantro-Lime Flounder
2	Creamy Keto Cucumber Salad	Peanut Butter and Jelly Grilled Sandwich	Minced Beef Samosa
3	Tasty Beef and Liver Burger	Crispy Lemon Chicken	Green Tuna Salad
4	Shredded Chicken Chili	Grilled Corn on the Cob	Meatloaf Sandwiches
5	Hot Fruit Salad	Cucumber Sandwich	Roasted Chicken and Vegetables
6	Bacon and Cheese Quiche	Ciabatta Rolls with Chicken Pesto	Salmon and Green Beans
7	Egg and Broccoli Casserole	Mexican Steak Tacos	Mango Cheesecake Smoothie
8	Berries and Cream Breakfast Cake	Marinated Shrimp Pasta Salad	Cucumber and Dill Cold Soup
9	Cabbage Goat Cheese and Chorizo Omelet	Pizza Pitas	Herb-Crusted Baked Haddock
10	Rice Milk	Beer Pork Ribs	Pizza Pitas
11	Mexican Style Burritos	Grilled Shrimp with Cucumber Lime Salsa	Baked Macaroni and Cheese
12	Blueberry Muffins	Eggplant Casserole	Beef Enchiladas
13	Berry Chia with Yogurt	Turkey Pinwheels	Eggplant Casserole

14	Cheesy Scrambled Egg with Fresh Herbs	Asparagus Fried Rice	Chicken Stew
15	Egg and Veggie Muffins	Shrimp Scampi Linguine	Simple Cabbage Soup
16	Turkey and Cabbage Scramble	Vegetable Minestrone	Cilantro and Chili Infused Swordfish
17	Bucket wheat and Grapefruit Porridge	Thai Fish Soup	Feta Bean Salad
18	Apple Pie	Chicken Tacos	Chicken and Savory Rice
19	Eggplant Chicken Sandwich	Curried Carrot and Beet Soup	Chicken and Broccoli Casserole
20	Panzanella Salad	Chicken and Broccoli Casserole	Couscous with Veggies
21	Chorizo Bowl with Corn	Vegetable Biryani	Pork Souvlaki
22	Eggs in Tomato Rings	Simple Chicken and Rice Soup	Cauliflower Rice
23	Arugula Eggs with Chili Peppers	Tuna Twist	Meatball Soup
24	Hot Cocoa	Mexican Chorizo Sausage	Sunny Pineapple Smoothie
25	Bulgur, Couscous and Bucket wheat Cereal	Pesto Pasta Salad	Mexican Chorizo Sausage
26	Poached Asparagus and Egg	Tuna Twist	Creamy Shells with Peas and Bacon
27	Cabbage and Ham Frittata	Grilled Onion and Pepper Jack Grilled Cheese Sandwich	Double-Boiled Stewed Potatoes
28	Blueberry Smoothie	Shrimp Quesadilla	Barley Blueberry Avocado Salad
29	Egg Drop Soup	Spicy Mushroom Stir-Fry	Taco Soup
30	Hot Fruit Salad	Pizza with Chicken and Pesto	Spicy Mushroom Stir-Fry
31	Rice Milk	Beer Pork Ribs	Pizza Pitas

MEASUREMENT COVERAGE CHART

Volume Equivalents (Liquid)

US STANDARD	US STANDARD (OUNCES)	METRIC (APPROXIMATE)
2 tablespoons	1 fl. oz.	30 mL
¼ cup	2 fl. oz.	60 mL
½ cup	4 fl. oz.	120 mL
1 cup	8 fl. oz.	240 mL
1½ cups	12 fl. oz.	355 mL
2 cups or 1 pint	16 fl. oz.	475 mL
4 cups or 1 quart	32 fl. oz.	1 L
1 gallon	128 fl. oz.	4 L

Oven Temperatures

FAHRENHEIT (F)	CELSIUS (C) (APPROXIMATE)
250°F	120°C
300°F	150°C
325°F	165°C
350°F	180°C
375°F	190°C
400°F	200°C
425°F	220°C
450°F	230°C

Volume Equivalents (Dry)

US STANDARD	METRIC (APPROXIMATE)
⅛ teaspoon	0.5 mL
¼ teaspoon	1 mL
½ teaspoon	2 mL
¾ teaspoon	4 mL
1 teaspoon	5 mL
1 tablespoon	15 mL
¼ cup	59 mL
⅓ cup	79 mL
½ cup	118 mL
⅔ cup	156 mL
¾ cup	177 mL
1 cup	235 mL
2 cups or 1 pint	475 mL
3 cups	700 mL
4 cups or 1 quart	1 L

Weight Equivalents

US STANDARD	METRIC (APPROXIMATE)
½ ounce	15 g
1 ounce	30 g
2 ounces	60 g
4 ounces	115 g
8 ounces	225 g
12 ounces	340 g
16 ounces or 1 pound	455 g

CONCLUSION

Thanks for your time. You have been given a big list of different recipes that you can start with when you have kidney problems. The recipes have been selected to be easy to follow and perfect for people who don't know a lot about cooking.

The renal diet is a diet that is designed to help people with chronic kidney disease or kidney failure. This means that the diet isn't an option for everyone, but it has shown some promising results in some people. The following are lessons learned from the renal diet so you can take it on before deciding whether it's right for you.

Remember that the best way to determine whether or not you can tackle the renal diet is by talking to your doctor. If you have no problems, then you should feel good about taking on this type of diet. Remember that you should never take on this type of diet if you are already in heart trouble, diabetes, or high blood pressure.

If you choose to take on the renal diet, no matter because you are doing it, be sure to make the most out of your journey. It is recommended to start slowing to get used to healthy eating habits. If things start easy enough for you, try adding a little more until you get used to the changes and stick with them.

You should try out as many of the recipes as possible to find ones that you enjoy. The more you practice cooking, the better you will get at it, and the more fun you will have with it.

If something doesn't work for you, don't give up just yet. Try a new recipe and keep practicing until you find a few that work for your body type.

Try to make a habit out of preparing a meal every day. There are some days when you don't have time to cook, but there are also some days when you will have no choice but to cook. Just make sure that it doesn't get in the way of your social life.

If you follow the recipes listed in this guide, you will get closer to living a healthier life with your kidney problems. You can also get back your life and prevent further complications from developing.

When you begin taking care of yourself and following the renal diet, you will notice results. You may even get rid of all of your symptoms completely.

The dietary changes that you wouldn't normally ever think about doing can help you get healthy and prevent further health problems from developing. You may also be able to live a healthier lifestyle that will serve you well in the future for your health and overall wellbeing.

Note that because everyone is different, the renal diet won't necessarily work for everyone. It can be annoying if this happens to you. You will then have to go back to doing what your doctor tells you that needs to be done and ultimately getting healthier than ever before.

ALPHABETICAL RECIPE INDEX

5

5 Ingredients Pasta _____ 87

A

Almond Milk _____ 106
Almond Pasta Salad _____ 81
American Blueberry Pancakes _____ 33
Apple and Strawberry Snack _____ 101
Arugula Eggs with Chili Peppers _____ 29
Asparagus Fried Rice _____ 77
Avocado Blueberry Cheesecake _____ 116
Azteca Cake _____ 111

B

Bake Pasta with Cashew Cream _____ 90
Baked Cod with Salsa _____ 67
Baked Fish à la Mushrooms _____ 61
Baked Flounder _____ 53
Baked Garlic _____ 39
Baked Macaroni and Cheese _____ 57
Baked Pineapple _____ 99
Baked Trout _____ 69
Balsamic Beet Salad _____ 80
Barbecue Meatballs _____ 41
Barley Blueberry Avocado Salad _____ 76
Basil Leaves Tea _____ 119
Beef Chili _____ 54
Beef Enchiladas _____ 58
Beer Pork Ribs _____ 44
Beet Feta Salad _____ 83
Berry Chia with Yogurt _____ 29
Blackberry Tea _____ 122
Blueberry Muffins _____ 28
Blueberry Smoothie _____ 106
Breakfast Maple Sausage _____ 32
Brie and Apple Salad _____ 82
Broccoli-Onion Latkes _____ 73
Buckwheat and Grapefruit Porridge ___ 28
Bulgur, Couscous, and Buckwheat Cereal
_____ 28
Butter-Orange Yams _____ 37
Butterscotch Apple Salad _____ 79

C

Cabbage Pear Salad _____ 82
Cabbage Rotelle Provençale _____ 95
Candied Macadamia Nuts _____ 102
Cannellini Pesto Spaghetti _____ 91
Caramel-Centered Cookies _____ 97
Carrot and Parsnips French Fries _____ 101

Carrot and Tofu Cake _____ 112
Carrot Cake _____ 112
Carrot Orange Ginger Smoothie _____ 107
Carrot Peach Water _____ 104
Carrot-Apple Casserole _____ 71
Cauliflower Rice _____ 73
Cheesy Broccoli Bites _____ 35
Cheesy Scrambled Eggs with Fresh Herbs
_____ 27
Cherry Limeade Smoothie _____ 107
Chicken and Broccoli Casserole _____ 59
Chicken and Savory Rice _____ 57
Chicken Cranberry Sauce Salad _____ 84
Chicken Orange Salad _____ 80
Chicken Stew _____ 55
Chicken Tacos _____ 48
Chocolate and Avocado Mousse _____ 115
Chocolate Mint Smoothie _____ 109
Chorizo Bowl with Corn _____ 30
Ciabatta Rolls with Chicken Pesto _____ 49
Cilantro and Chili Infused Swordfish ___ 68
Cilantro-Lime Flounder _____ 67
Cinnamon Apple Chips _____ 102
Citrus Tuna Ceviche _____ 68
Coconut Chia Pudding _____ 116
Cold Orange Soba Noodles _____ 91
Cooked Tilapia with Mango Salsa _____ 68
Cool Avocado Pudding _____ 115
Couscous Burgers _____ 52
Couscous with Veggies _____ 47
Crab Cakes with Lime Salsa _____ 65
Crab-Stuffed Celery Logs _____ 40
Cranberry Cabbage _____ 73
Cranberry Slaw _____ 79
Cream of Watercress _____ 38
Creamed Chicken Salad _____ 83
Creamy Cucumber _____ 40
Creamy Pumpkin Pasta _____ 90
Creamy Shells with Peas _____ 71
Creamy Spinach Pasta _____ 91
Creamy Vegan Mushroom Pasta _____ 88
Crispy Lemon Chicken _____ 43
Crispy Tofu and Vegetable Noodles ____ 92
Cucumber and Lemon-Flavored Water 106
Cucumber Sandwich _____ 47
Cucumber-Carrot Salad _____ 84
Curried Fish Cakes _____ 69
Curried Veggies and Rice _____ 74

D

Dates and Rice Pudding _____ 115
Dessert Pizza _____ 98
Dill Nibbles _____ 40
Double-Boiled Country Style Fried
Potatoes _____ 72
Double-Boiled Stewed Potatoes _____ 72

E

Easy Caprese Skewers _____ 35
Easy Caramel Apple Salad _____ 86
Easy Egg Salad _____ 47
Easy No-Bake Coconut Cookies _____ 103
Egg and Veggie Fajitas _____ 75
Egg and Veggie Muffins _____ 29
Egg Celery Salad _____ 80
Egg Drop Soup _____ 32
Egg White and Broccoli Omelet _____ 34
Eggplant and Red Pepper Soup _____ 51
Eggplant Casserole _____ 45
Eggplant Chicken Sandwich _____ 30
Eggplant Seafood Casserole _____ 63
Eggs in Tomato Rings _____ 30
Elderflower Tea _____ 121

F

Farfalle Confetti Salad _____ 82
Fast Microwave Egg Scramble _____ 33
Fennel Tea _____ 121
Feta Bean Salad _____ 59
Flax Seed Tea _____ 119
Fresh Fruit Dessert Cups _____ 96

G

Garlic Mashed Potatoes _____ 70
Garlicky Penne Pasta with Asparagus __ 70
Ginger Glazed Carrots _____ 71
Ginger Onion Tea _____ 120
Grapes Jicama Salad _____ 79
Green Apple Orange Spice _____ 108
Green Beans in Oven _____ 38
Green Tea Pudding _____ 114
Green Tuna Salad _____ 55
Grilled Corn on the Cob _____ 46
Grilled Onion and Pepper Jack Grilled
Cheese Sandwich _____ 50
Grilled Shrimp with Cucumber Lime Salsa
_____ 65
Grilled Tofu with Sesame Seeds _____ 35
Ground Beef and Rice Soup _____ 52
Guava Tea _____ 119

H

Halibut with Lemon Caper Sauce _____ 63
Healthy Green Smoothie _____ 107
Healthy Spiced Nuts _____ 100
Herb-Crusted Baked Haddock _____ 66
Hibiscus Green Tea _____ 119

Hibiscus Raspberry Green Tea _____ 121
Holiday Cheese Ball _____ 41
Holiday Cider _____ 104
Holiday Tuna Ball _____ 42
Hot Cocoa _____ 105
Hula Meatballs _____ 42

I

Indonesia Green Noodle Salad _____ 93
Italian Meatballs _____ 44

J

Jambalaya _____ 64
Jicama and Carrot Salad with Honey-Lime
  Dressing _____ 85

K

Kale Chips _____ 36
Kidney-Friendly Vanilla Ice Cream _____ 99
Kimchi Green Rice Noodle Salad _____ 93
Korean Pear Salad _____ 58

L

Lavender Tea _____ 118
Layered Smoothie _____ 107
Lemon Bars _____ 98
Lemon Cake _____ 114
Lemon Ginger Tea _____ 123
Lemon Meringue Pie _____ 96
Lemon Pops _____ 102
Lemony Broccoli Penne _____ 93
Lettuce Wraps with Chicken _____ 50
Licorice Tea for Energy Boost _____ 122
Low-Sodium Lb. Cake _____ 97
Luscious Lemon Tea _____ 122

M

Mango Cheesecake Smoothie _____ 105
Mango Coconut Cheesecake _____ 116
Mango Coconut Pudding _____ 117
Maple Fig Smoothie _____ 108
Marinated Shrimp Pasta Salad _____ 49
Mediterranean Couscous Salad _____ 85
Mexican Chorizo Sausage _____ 44
Mexican Nibbles _____ 39
Mexican Scrambled Eggs in Tortilla _____ 33

Mexican Steak Tacos _____ 43
Mexican Style Burritos _____ 45
Mint Protein: Smoothie _____ 108
Morning Turmeric Tonic _____ 122

O

Old Fashioned Salmon Soup _____ 62
Orange and Chocolate Cake _____ 112

P

Panzanella Salad _____ 31
Papaya Mint Water _____ 104
Pasta with Creamy Broccoli Sauce _____ 77
Peachy Keen Smoothie _____ 109
Peanut Butter and Jelly Grilled Sandwich
  _____ 49
Pear Basil Citrus Smoothie _____ 109
Peppermint Crunch Cookies _____ 99
Peppermint Tea _____ 118
Persian Chicken _____ 53
Pesto Pasta Salad _____ 76
Pineapple Berry Salad _____ 81
Pineapple Shrimp Salad _____ 86
Pizza Pitas _____ 48
Pizza with Chicken and Pesto _____ 45
Plant-Based Keto Lo Mein _____ 87
Poached Egg with Asparagus _____ 31
Ponzu Pea Rice Noodle Salad _____ 94
Poppy Seeds Tea _____ 120
Pork Meatloaf _____ 54
Pork Souvlaki _____ 53
Potato and Mushroom Cake _____ 111
Powerhouse Green Tea _____ 123

Q

Quick Cupcakes _____ 99

R

Raspberry Cucumber Smoothie _____ 105
Raspberry Overnight Porridge _____ 32
Rice Milk _____ 106
Roasted Asparagus and Red Peppers _____ 37
Roasted Chicken and Vegetables _____ 56
Roasted Chili-Vinegar Peanuts _____ 103
Roasted Delicata Squash with Thyme _____ 37
Roasted Tomato Brussels Sprouts _____ 38
Rose chamomile Tea _____ 118

S

Salmon and Green Beans _____ 57
Salmon Mayo Sandwich _____ 60
Sautéed Collard Greens and Cabbage _ 36
Sautéed Green Beans _____ 70
Seafood Casserole _____ 51
Sesame Crackers _____ 100
Shiitake and Bean Sprout Ramen _____ 94
Shiitake Udon Noodles _____ 95
Shrimp and Asparagus Linguine _____ 61
Shrimp in Garlic Sauce _____ 62
Shrimp Quesadilla _____ 46
Shrimp Scampi Linguine _____ 65
Shrimp Szechuan _____ 64
Simple Deviled Eggs _____ 36
Sirloin Medallions, Green Squash, and
  Pineapple _____ 56
Spice Cake _____ 114
Spicy Mushroom Stir-Fry _____ 74
Spicy Sweet Chili Veggie Noodles _____ 88
Spicy Veggie Pancakes _____ 74
Stir Fry Noodles _____ 88
Strawberry Biscuit Cake _____ 110
Stress Relief Tea _____ 123
Summer Veggie Omelet _____ 32
Sunny Pineapple Smoothie _____ 105
Sweet Glazed Salmon _____ 66

T

Tarragon and Pepper Pasta Salad _____ 83
Tarragon Spring Peas _____ 37
Tofu and Chocolate Mousse _____ 113
Tuna Twist _____ 63
Turkey and Spinach Scramble on Melba
  Toast _____ 27
Turkey Pinwheels _____ 48
Turmeric Tea _____ 120

V

Vegan Chinese Noodles _____ 89
Vegan Chocolate Peanut Butter
  Cheesecake _____ 110
Vegan Chocolate Pudding _____ 113
Vegan Corn Cake _____ 110
Vegetable Biryani _____ 75
Vegetable Penne Pasta _____ 89
Vegetarian Taco Salad _____ 78
Veggie Noodles _____ 87
Veggie Snack _____ 100
Vinegar and Salt Kale Chips _____ 101

Printed in Great Britain
by Amazon

16534041R00075